From Trial to Testimony

By Christine Gulley Kirk

From Trial to Testimony

By Christine Kirk

Copyright © 2013
Christine Gulley-Kirk

All rights reserved under international copyright laws. With the exception of brief quotes in reviews or articles, no Portion of this book may be reproduced in any form, print, digital, audio or video, without the express written consent of the author.

Voice of the Spirit Media Group
Auburn Hills, Michigan

Table of Contents

Foreword		4
Acknowledgments		5
Introduction		7
1.	The Day My Life Changed	9
2.	A Cry for Help	19
3.	The Abuse	28
4.	The Rape	50
5.	Trusting the Wrong People	61
6.	What Was I Thinking	71
7.	A Motherless Child	83
8.	All Things Must End	88
9.	Getting My Life Back	97
10.	Freedom	104

Foreword
By Dr. Gregory Heathman

Love all of God's Word but like most people, I have a few select passages that really resonate with me. Among them is Revelation 12:1; *"And they overcame him by the blood of the Lamb, and by the word of their testimony..."*

A testimony is the story told by one who was there; One who witnessed the events first hand. A testimony is evidence produced by one who has first hand, experiential knowledge of the power of God.

In this book, the author shares her testimony in startling detail. She withholds nothing. She boldly and courageously lays her life open like a book and allows us to read every page, the good, the bad and the ugly.

She is painfully honest and brutally frank as she shares the story of her descent into the depths of despair and degradation. She is poignant and inspiring as she shares the story of her climb out of the dungeon of misery back to the mountaintop of God's mercy and grace.

Christine makes no effort to be churchy or to protect our religious sensibilities. It is the raw, straight forward, telling of one woman's journey from victim to victory. More than that, it assures us all that no one is ever so lost that Jesus cannot find him, save him and use him mightily.

Acknowledgements

I must start by giving thanks to God. He is everything to me. Without Him, I do not know where I would be. I thank God for loving me and proving that his love for me is truly unconditional. I thank him for entrusting me to minister to his people and for allowing me to be one of his chosen vessels.

To my husband Avery, I love you more than words can ever express. Thank you for being patient with me and for standing by me through all my pain and mess. Thank you for pushing me when I wanted to give up. Most of all thank you for being my best friend.

My babies Jeremiah, Khrystiana and Asia mommy loves you very much.

My parents I thank God for the time I shared with my mother Donna Marie, she was my hero. She is and always will be, missed. To my father, I love you very much you have always been there for me no matter what. I don't know what I would do without my daddy!

To my spiritual mother and father, Pastors Gregory and Patricia Heathman, you have always been there for me. I do not know what I would do if it were not for your encouraging words. Thank you for loving me enough to keep me in line and for never giving up on me. Thanks for always being willing to lend an ear when I need to yell and vent, thank you for allowing me to use what God has given me under your leadership.

To my godmother, Sylathia Hollie, I thank God

for you, you know more about me than a lot of people yet you have never judged me. Thank you for allowing me to be a part of your life.

Last, but not least, to all my siblings Catherine Gulley, Melissa Gulley, Caleb Gulley, Jo Ann Gulley, Allen Gulley and Jessica Gulley I love you all. Thanks for all your support and for putting up with my big, loud mouth.

Introduction

God spoke to me a year ago and told me to write a book. A year ago, I was fresh in the healing process. I did not understand why he would tell me to do such a thing. I felt it was much too early. I did not understand why He felt I was ready for such a task. In fact, I was not even close to being ready.

I, at that time, did not understand the love and mercy of God. I did not understand that God could bless your mess. I didn't even feel like I was worthy of what he had planned for me. I thought my life would be hell until the day I die.

The journey that God had for me was too much for me to believe. Not me, I was not the one God was going to prosper! Heck no, I had too much going on and too much healing to go through!

On top of that, I was still in sin. What was God thinking? "Does He know who I am? Does He know that I am filthy? Did He not see what I did? What's wrong with Him?" I would ask myself. I am sure many of you have asked the same questions.

I did not believe in myself. My self-esteem was low. I was not perfect enough and I definitely was not as good as everyone else.

I was loud, always the tallest, skinny, out spoken, blunt, creative and silly these things are all fine right? Not to me, I always felt bad about being different. All I wanted was to fit in so I could feel like I belonged even if it meant risking my reputation. As long as I was just like those around me that would not matter.

No matter how hard I tried to fit in I always felt different. I could be around a room full of people and still I would always feel different. All my life I was different I have known many people in my life but I still have never found anyone quite like me.

I was ashamed of who I was. Instead of walking in who God said I was, I walked in who the enemy led me to believe that I was.

I was broken, unhappy, always depressed, stressed, hurt, bitter, angry and frustrated. I felt like I needed to be in a mental institution. One more thing, one more time, I was going to snap! I was at my breaking point!

Have you ever felt this way? Have you ever wondered why you could never be in the popular crowd? Have you ever wondered why it was that you were- given the short end of the stick? Does it seem like you are always going through some trial when everyone else is smiling, happy and seem to be prospering. Why are people so much harder on you than they are on everyone else? Have you ever thought that maybe it is all a part of the process? Maybe, you are not just called, you are chosen!

If you can relate to this, you and I have a lot in common. As Christians, we are not called to fit in but to stand out. God is trying to take you from trial to testimony.

Chapter 1
The Day My Life Changed

It was July 15, 2003 about 8:00 AM., a Tuesday morning.

I will never forget it. My sisters and I were at my Grandma's house preparing to go see my mother in the hospital. I was downstairs in the bedroom. I had been up all night. I just could not sleep knowing that my mother was not at home with us. I was wrestling with denial.

I have always been prophetic. Even as a little kid, God would allow me to see things. I knew when someone was about to die. God would give me a dream that would prepare me for the bad news. God gave me a dream, weeks prior to this day, a dream that my mother would die. I ignored it and marked it as a dream from Satin. My mother would surly live God would not allow her to die, it was not time.

As I sat up all night, I cried to God asking and begging him not to allow my mother to die. "Lord I will do anything!" I cried out "Just please Lord please don't allow my mother to die!"

I felt so helpless, there was part of me that would say God is going to answer my prayer but almost all of me knew she was not coming back home. I still held on to the little bit of hope I did have, and then I heard a knock at the door. It was two of my family members coming to pick my sisters, grandma and me up to go see my mother. I rushed up the stairs but about half way to the top of the staircase, I saw my grandma in tears.

My aunt stood at the top of the stairs looking at me with a look of despair. My heart dropped to the floor. I quietly asked, "Is she dead"? She nodded, yes. I screamed from the very bottom of my soul! "NO!" I screamed "why, how?" I asked.

I ran down the stairs grabbed my mother's picture and held it tight. It was at that moment that I decided I was never going to let her go.

I felt so betrayed by God and as crazy as it sounds, I felt betrayed by my mother too. I was angry, sad, frustrated, scared, shocked and worried all at once. I was only 18. I was experiencing things I had never felt before. I just wanted to lay beside my mother and die. Without her, there was no reason for me to live.

I looked up toward the ceiling and yelled at God "I will never serve you again!" I meant every word I spoke. I begged and I cried for God to spare my mother's life and he did not listen! I was so angry I wanted to kill everyone at the hospital. I had never been so angry in all my life! This anger was real I was enraged.

At that moment, something in me changed. I was no longer sweet, loud, funny Christine. My spirit was officially dead, my heart turned cold and the love I once had for God was gone. I hated Him with every part of my spirit, soul and body. From this day forward, I will take matters in to my own hands; those who know me know that once I make it up in my mind, that's it!

As I sat there, I began to think of ways I could have helped. The more I thought about it, the more I realized, this was all my fault. You see, on the Sunday before all of this I saw my mother at the hospital and she was fine. She was sitting up in her bed talking to me and every- thing seemed normal. I asked her could I stay that night with her and she told me no. When she told me no, some- thing did not sit right in my spirit.

As we left the hospital, I began to cry because something deep, down on the inside of me did not feel right. The next day, my mother was unconscious. I felt that if I had been there I could have saved her. The last picture I have of my mother, she is lying in a hospital bed with her eyes rolled back, a tube in her mouth with fluid coming out of it. Little did I know this picture would be the very cause of many problems to come!

After sitting at my grandmas for a while, we left and went to the home of another family member. I re- member thinking, "Who can I call?" someone who could relate to how I was feeling. The only person who could always understand me was my mother and she was dead. I felt empty on the inside, my body was weak, my head was hurting from all the tears and my heart was broken.

I did not know what my sisters and I were going to do or where we would go. I could not imagine a good life without my mother. Although I had my sisters and my family, without my mother, I felt completely alone. I would cry and then stop in shock! I felt as if I was having a nightmare. I just knew I would wake up, and all this madness would be over. My mother was going to walk in the door at any moment and we would all laugh and talk the way we always did.

As the day went on, I began to realize that my mother Donna Marie Gulley was never ever coming back! I got no sleep that night. I was too busy crying. I was truly grieved. The more I cried the more I died.

The next few days, the house, as you could imagine, was full of people who loved my mother and who claimed they would be there for my sisters and I.

Everything made me upset I did not want people hugging on me to much or telling me it was Ok. Everyone, at that point, was an enemy. I trusted no one, after all God had let me down so I knew people would let me down too. I just wanted to kill myself.

The devil immediately came in and took hold of my mind. I did not want to go another second without my mother. I began to believe that if I were to kill myself I would be with her. I thought of many ways to kill myself but could not come up with anything that would not hurt. I was to "chicken" to get the job done.

There were times when I wanted to laugh, smile, or just feel joyful but those moments were few and fleeting as feelings of betrayal and guilt, would suddenly sweep over me, because my mother had just passed. "There was no way I could be happy after my mom just suffered such a horrible death," I thought to myself. I felt like I had no choice but to sit and be miserable and since that is what I believed, that is what I did.

I did not take showers. I did not do my hair. I did not want to do anything. What I wanted was to go to sleep and never wake up again.

When we would leave the house and see other

people with their mothers, I would get very emotional or angry. I would begin to ask God, "Why not their mother? Why mine?" I would think about all the people I went to high school with and how some of them would complain because their mother was on crack or was not even in the home. Why, should those mothers be allowed to live and my mother, a woman who loved the Lord with all her heart, not strung out on drugs, not sleeping around, a true woman of God, should die. So again I ask God, "Why my mother?" I just did not understand it.

My mother made sure we were taken care of she took us shopping, She made sure we got our hair done every two weeks. We did not always have all the things we wanted but she made sure we had all that we needed.

My mother did not play when it came to her girls, Catherine, Melissa and me. Those who knew her knew that if you messed with her girls she was going to get in your mix.

My mother was a diva. Her hair and nails stayed done, she stayed sharp in her suits and matching high heels and she would top it off with a nice scarf and her bright red lipstick.

My mother was strong. I admired her strength. At times, she would be going through so much but still managed to take care of three girls.

My mother was no joke she did not play! If I dared talked back, she would grab a hold of me and I would know I have said too much. It makes me smile, now, when I think about it.

My mother and I were so much alike. Often we would clash. Sometimes, my mother would tell me, "Christine when you come in the room it's like a light, you just brighten up my day!" Then she would smile, I would, as well. I would sit next to her and she would hold me.

I even remember a time my boyfriend Keith and I got into an argument I got off the phone in tears, my mother let me lay on her and just cry as she rubbed my head. That is a memory I will always carry with me because it was at that moment that I felt secure, loved and safe. My mother without a shadow of doubt loved my sisters and me. My mother proved that, yes, single par- ting is hard but it can be done.

One year, around Christmas time, my mother told my sister and me that we might not get anything for Christmas that year because she did not have the money. Though we were sad, we understood and we did not want to cause my mother anymore pain by complaining. She was already in tears. We all hugged our mother kissed her and told her it was ok. That Christmas I do not know how she did it, we had everything we asked for and we were so excited. She made it happen I will never forget that, we had some good times with our mother and we had some bad times as well.

I was the rebellious sister. I wanted to do what I wanted to do and go where I wanted to go. I became very good at sneaking around when my mother would drop me off to school when I was in the tenth grade I would leave and skip school with my friends. One day when I left with my best friend Julie we went to a guy's house that I really liked one thing led to another and I lost my virginity at sixteen years old. Three days later, I ran across a guy who I dated in ninth grade. He had cheated on me with my cousin because, at the time, I was not sexually active. I had sex with him just because I had lost my virginity and I was excited.

I began skipping school on a regular basis to have sex with him. I ended up telling my older sister Catherine and she told my mother.

My mother called me in the room. As she cried, I sat next to her thinking she was going to slap the crap out of me at any time. To my surprise she started laughing I was in shock I looked at her and said, "Mama what is so funny"? She said, "Christine you are just like your mother." I just smiled, apologized for my actions and promised never to do it again.

When I got back in my room, I was so relieved that I was not in pain from my mother knocking me out.

A few months after that, I decided to step my game up and have him, come to my house.

That morning, as we were leaving for school, I made sure I was the last one out. That way I could make sure the door was left unlocked.

That day, I slipped out of school, my friend came and picked me up and we went to my house. We were just talking and joking around, nothing sexual had occurred, when I heard a noise outside. I rushed to the window. It was my godmother! I was so scared! I did not know what to do. We both ran into my sister's closet to hide. When my god-mother came in, she called out, "Hello," as if she knew someone was in the house. She walked straight into the room where I was hiding and opened the door. I knew then I was about to get it.

She asked what I was doing there and told me she was telling my mother. I was so terrified I began thinking of ways to run away. I did not want to face the wrath of my mother.

Once my mom got home, she took her heels off and came straight for me. She yelled and yanked me up then made me get the boy on the telephone. She told him that if he ever called me or came near me again, he was going to jail.

After that I was on a strict punishment I could not do anything.

The last memory I have of my mother, alive and well was the week before she died. My mother had told me to do something. I did not want to do it so I back talked her in a disrespectful way.

That week I was going to Florida, to Disney World, with my cousins. She told me I could not go because of my mouth. I was so upset; she called and told my uncle. He talked her in to allowing me to go. I bought my mother a card and a mug. I could not wait to give it to her.

We got back to Michigan on a Sunday. That is when I saw my mother at the hospital. The next day she was unconscious and that Tuesday she was dead. I never got a chance to tell her that I was sorry for all I had done. I never got a chance to tell her how much I loved her and how much I was going to miss her. What hurt the most is I never got a chance to say goodbye.

Never take your mother for granted. Cherish each moment you have with her. Each moment, good or bad, is a gift. I wish my mother were still here, jacking me up and yelling at me. I wish she could be here to punish me when I act up. Those times count and they mean the world to you once she is gone. Respect your mother. Do not allow friends, family and boyfriends to cause you to disrespect the woman that brought you into this world.

Our mothers have a story as well they do not always share it and they are not always right. There is a reason you were raised the way you were raised. You are angry with your mother and it is not her fault. Let it go! It was God's plan!

I say to those who do not have a relationship with your mother, if she is still alive; stop waiting for her to make it right. You make it right before it is too late. Forgive her, let it go. Move on with your life. I do not know whom that was for but I pray that God would heal your wounds and heal the relationship with you and your mother; in Jesus precious name Amen.

To those who never knew your mother or lost her before you had a chance to established a relationship with her, God said, in Isaiah 66:13, "As a mother com- forts her son, so will I comfort you." Allow God to fill the emptiness you feel. Let him comfort you and hold you. He will do it. He is waiting for you. Yes you! He is saying, "My arms are open wide and I have never left your side. Even when you thought I abandoned you I was right beside you."

He loves you! I feel the Holy Spirit all over me right now, as I write! Be free woman of God and let the

Lord be your healer, In Jesus Name, Amen! I am rejoicing with you thank God for freedom!

Chapter 2
Family Feuds

The memory of me back talking my mother and not being able to apologize was a weight I carried day after day. I felt horrible. I felt like my mother died because she was tired of me talking back. I just wanted to tell her I was sorry and that I loved her. I felt like that moment was taken from me and it was Gods fault.

I began to feel very sick; a type of sickness I had never experienced before. With everything going on, I did not even realize I had missed my period not for just 1 month but for 2 months! "I could not be pregnant!" I thought. "It had only been about 3 days since I buried my mother! God wouldn't allow this to happen to me too." "Yes!" Everything was God's fault even though it was my choice to sleep around without protection; it was all Gods fault.

I needed to figure out how I could get a pregnancy test without my uncle or aunt knowing. I decided that if I were pregnant I was going to abort it so they surely could not find out.

The next day my older sister Catherine and I went to the mall to meet up with a friend. I told Catherine and my friend what was going on. To my surprise, my girlfriend was having the same issue. She and I decided to take a test together. I had a feeling I was pregnant I just did not want to believe that all this could happen to me at once. I did not have these kinds of issues when my mom was alive. When my mother was alive, my biggest issue was what I was going to wear to school the next morning.

We both went to the restroom to take the test. When we saw the results, I was not surprised. POSITIVE! Both of us were pregnant!

I just wanted to fall out and die! God what did I do to deserve all this. As far as I was concerned, God was the first person on my hate list. He has too much power to allow all this to happen to me. Give me a break GOD!

My sister did not make it any better all she could say was "you'd better be glad mama is not here. She would kill you!"

All I could think about was what my dad and uncle would say. I wanted to abort the baby but how do you do that with no car and no money?

As soon as I returned to my uncle's house, I grabbed the phone book and began looking up abortion clinics. I had to figure out how much it would cost and what I would have to go through.

After looking up all the information, I decided I just could not do it. It was too much money and the process was just too traumatic for me. Now it was time to figure out how to tell my father and uncle. I told my cousins what was going on and they thought it would be best if I had my aunt tell my uncle.

While at church on that following Sunday, my cousin and a friend of the family, pulled my aunt aside and told her I was pregnant. She already knew! The lord had already revealed it to her. She was not angry; she smiled and said it would be a boy. "What a relief," I thought to myself.

That was the easy part. My aunt told me I would have to tell my uncle once we got home. Once service was over and we were on our way home, I thought I was going to pass out from all the anxiety I was having over the idea of telling my uncle and my dad. Once we got to the house, I told my uncle I had something to tell him. My aunt, uncle and I went into the office and I just let it out.

He began asking questions about the father of the baby. I assured him that Keith was a good person, that he loved me with all his heart, and that he was going to take care of his baby. I was confident. I knew I had a man that was going to support me, and my child. No one was going to tell me any different. "I am grown I got this." Later on, I discovered that all I had was a hard head and a big mouth. Once I told Keith, I was pregnant, everything changed and I do mean everything.

I only talked to Keith on the phone and that was only when I called him. He would ask me for money. Remember, now, my mother had just died and I was pregnant with his baby! He never once asked how the baby or I was doing but you still could not tell me that he did not love me. I told him, as soon as I got some money I would give it to him. He would say, "I love you," I would say it back and just melt.

One day my uncle gave my sisters and me some money so we could go to the mall. I called Keith and told him to meet me at the mall. I had some money. I gave him $200 because he said he had to get his car fixed. I loved him and knew he just loved me to pieces. I wanted to help him. I loved Keith so much I would have given him everything I had, if he had asked for it. One time, I went shopping for him. I bought him some under wear, socks and other things. When I arrived at his house to give them to him, there was a girl upstairs! I was very upset but not at Keith, I was mad at the girl. That is Crazy, right?

I yelled up the stairs and told her she had better be gone when I got back and told him the same. Like an idiot, I left, giving him ample time to do as he pleased with the girl before she left. Once I returned I was so happy, she was not there. I was in the presence of my dream lover.

I would go over to Keith's house often to have sex. Many times he would leave me there and be elsewhere, but I did not care. I just knew that he loved me too much to be with someone else even though the girl I mentioned earlier was there. He would never sleep with someone else! I was so caught up in this man I could have seen him in the act of cheating and I still would not have believed it was him.

That would all change at my next doctor's visit. I had been experiencing some vaginal itching and burning and the discharge that was coming out was not normal! The doctor checked me out and to my surprise; I had an STD, Trichomoniasis!

You would have thought the doc told me I had HIV the way I reacted to that news! I was shocked, scared, angry and worried about my unborn baby.

I went over to Keith's house while he was in school and waited. I was so angry I did not know what to do with myself. When he walked in, he was shocked to see me. I had never come over without him knowing first.

I told him that we needed to talk and we went upstairs I told him what the doctors said, and to my even greater surprise, He blamed me!

Can you believe that? The nerve of him, to accuse me of cheating, I would never have done such a thing. I loved him right down to his dirty socks. I pleaded with him not to lie to me and he finally came out with the truth. As crazy, as it sounds I was crushed. I liked it better when he was lying to me. I just did not want to believe he would do that to me. How he could do that and not think about protecting me was just beyond me.

I was just so hurt I did not know what to do. My mother was dead. There was no one I felt I could talk to so I buried that hurt deep inside and tried to move on.

I was 18 years old and already my life was headed in the wrong direction. I did not care about myself I did not even know who I was. I allowed others to define me and I did all I could to fit their definition even if it meant humiliating myself. I just wanted to fill the empty void on the inside of me and I was determined that Keith would be the one to fill it.

After losing my mother and now with a baby on the way, I was a stressed mess! My little sister Melissa was also under stress she and was only fifteen years old when my mother passed and she was miserable.

We shared a room at my uncle's house. At times, we would both sit and cry. I felt like she was my responsibility. My older sister Catherine felt as if Melissa and I both were her responsibility.

I loved living in Pontiac, now we were in one of the more affluent suburbs outside of Detroit. It was a place where people act as if food stamps are a germ. I wanted to leave so bad. Do not get me wrong, the house was beautiful, the people were nice enough, the neighborhood was pleasant but it just was not home to me.

There were many arguments with my sisters and other family members. I was always on edge. I was, still dealing with the grief of losing my mother, It seemed as if some of my family and close friends did not get it. Everyone had moved on with life as if nothing had happened. That made me angry. I felt as if they had all for- gotten my mother. They were treating her as if she did not matter.

At the time, I did not understand that everyone deals with things differently. I felt as if they did not care about my sisters and I and our needs. It seemed they were not concerned about how to make us comfortable as we dealt with the tragedy of our mother's death.

We had beds, food and clothing; the necessities we just did not have any part of the life we had with our mother. Without her, everything was so different; so unfamiliar.

Pontiac had been our home and our comfort zone. Our support system of friends and close family were there. The church that we had grown up in was in Pontiac.

When my mother died, we were told that we would be able to continuing going to our church, in Pontiac. After the funeral that all changed. They did not even want us in Pontiac!

My sister Melissa and I were furious. I really wanted to see my godmother. She and my mother were like sisters. I felt that she would understand. Perhaps, she missed mom as much as I did. Perhaps she would know what to say to help me deal with the pain. She loved me as if I was her very own daughter. I knew she could and would help me.

At first, I could not get why she was not coming around to see me. Later, I found out that she had tried but some of my family members kept her away.

I felt as if my own church family had forgotten about us. I needed to be embraced, I needed to feel loved I needed a void filled and I felt like there was no one I could turn to. I was eighteen years old and pregnant. I did not know what to do with myself. I know my mother would have been upset about me being pregnant but she still would have been there for me. That is all I wanted. Although I knew no one could take her place I was willing to try to find someone or something close to fill the emptiness I was feeling.

I also felt like a walking bank account. It seemed as if some people were more interested in my mother's life insurance than in us. I hated it. I just wanted to scream!

My father was angry! He felt betrayed because we did not want to live with him. My father can be a bit overbearing at times. My sisters and I were in that time of life when young people want a little freedom. We wanted to hang out with our friends and stay out late at night but my father would have a problem with that.

We love our father and we know he loves us but his strict, regimented lifestyle is a bit much for three young women coming into adulthood.

One day I was on the phone and my cousin wanted to use it. I told him to wait but for whatever reason, he felt that I needed to get off right then. I was pregnant with my son and my cousin attempted to grab the phone hitting me in my face in his attempt.

I was furious. We began fighting. One of my family members came home just in time to break up the fight. She asked why we could not get along. We were always into it. I did not like him. That is when it came out. I yelled, "Because he touched me!

My cousin got very upset and tried to hit me but others in the room held him back. As is often the case in these situations, no one wants to believe such a thing. Everyone wants to believe the victim is mistaken, exaggerating or making it up. As the victim, I can tell you that it makes you feel as if you are being violated all over again.

I wish my mother had said something about it when she was alive. She said she did not know what to do, so she did nothing.

I do not fault her for it now. I just wonder where it started.

That was the last time that situation came up until I went to my grandmother's house.

My aunt Francis came to me, gave me a big hug and said, "Christine I believe you." I will never forget that moment. I just stood there in her embrace and cried.

After moving out, I lived from house-to-house. Eventually, I moved back in with my dad. At first, everything was cool; he did not care what time we came in. He was never there, himself.

Things were going really well. My sister Melissa moved in to my dad's house as well.

Chapter 3
The Abuse

I had not taken a good breath when all the drama with Keith began. Keith and I were on and off throughout my pregnancy. We argued a lot. I figured that was normal. We would get through an argument, kiss, make up and move on.

Keith really changed, as our arguments got bigger and worse. He would begin to say hurtful things to me. I did not love myself so, to me, it really did not matter. I felt he was right.

He began calling my phone more often. I thought it was because he was worried about the baby and me. After all, I was still pregnant. He would tell me where I should and should not go, whom he liked in my life and whom he did not. I thought all this was because my man loved me.

I called him one day extra excited because I had come up with a name for the baby. I wanted his name to be Jeremiah because my mother's first-born was a boy and his name was Jeremiah. He had been stillborn and my mother always wanted another boy. I thought Keith would understand how much it meant to me to name my son Jeremiah but I was wrong. He told me that if I did not name his son after him the baby was not his. Even his family had the nerve to get involved on his side.

Now let me take the time to explain myself. I know family will stick together, but I had been raised to believe, right is right and wrong is wrong no matter who is doing it. In this case, Keith was dead wrong! Not for wanting a junior but for the way, he went about telling me.

I yelled at him and hung up in his face. I was just so angry. I hated that I was dumb enough to lay-down and have a baby with such a jerk. Keith was not at all who I thought he was. He was rude, mean, inconsiderate and so much more.

At the time, I was living with my father and I hated being there. My dad was just so strict and had too many rules. I became very rebellious. I wanted to do what I wanted to do! I did not want anyone to stop me or have anything to say about it.

My dad and I had always had a strained relationship. From as early as I can remember, we always seemed to clash over one thing or another.

All the hurt and pain I had suppressed was coming to surface all at once and I did not know how to contain myself. One day I lied to my dad. I told him I was going to stay the night with a friend when, in reality, that friend was Keith. That night, as Keith was driving me home to get a change of clothes we got into another argument. I do not remember what the argument was about. As I recall, it was not that serious. Most of our arguments were dumb and pointless.

This particular night things went too far! Keith slapped me! I could not believe he had just put his hands on me! I was shocked and hurt. I remember crying and asking him, "Why?" He looked at me as if he did not mean to do it. He told me he did not mean it and I believed him.

The tables turned quickly. I was the one who had just been slapped, but somehow he was the victim.

I asked him was he OK and told him, "I know you didn't mean it." We kissed and made up and everything was fine.

January 2, 2004 my son Jeremiah was born. I was so happy and so scared at the same time! I had no clue how to raise a child. A part of me wanted to give him up to someone who I knew would take care of him but the other part of me could not give him up. I thought once my baby was born that Keith and I would grow closer but we only fell apart.

Keith took advantage of the fact that I could not have sex for 6 weeks and used it as an excuse to sleep around.

My baby was not even in this world a month when Keith began acting like a fool.

I began looking at my baby and feeling so sorry for him, because I had brought him into this world while I was jacked up myself and his dad was a jerk.

Keith was already starting to prove that he did not intend to be a good father. Once my six weeks of no sex was up I immediately had sex with Keith, I felt if he had me there was no reason for him to have another chick. I got pregnant a second time! Not even two whole months after Jeremiah was born.

There was no way I was having another baby! I did not want to kill it. I feared something would happen to me if I aborted the baby. I was so self-centered. On the other hand, I did not want to have the baby because I could barely take care of Jeremiah. Besides, what would the people at church say? They were already talking about my son, because he had been born less than a year after my mother's passing. The embarrassment, the shame; I just could not take it.

Once my welfare money came in and with a little help from a friend, I got an abortion. It was the craziest thing I had ever done! I felt horrible seeing my innocent baby sucked out of my body into a bottle!

I told no one but my sisters, my cousin and of course Keith.

Once back at home, I began to experience pain in my stomach that was every bit as bad as contractions. I could not even breathe. I called my cousin. She rushed me to the hospital. The doctors could not figure out what was wrong. I ended up staying in the hospital for several days. Once released, I still had no understanding as to why I felt so much pain.

After having the abortion, I went through a lot of emotional torment. I lost weight. I went from a size seven to a size three in only a few months. I was only 120 pounds at 6'0 tall. I was totally unhealthy. I needed help. I did not know what to do or who to turn to. The only time I ate anything was after smoking weed. Marijuana always gave me the munchies. I did not know, at the time, that I was suffering from (PAS) Post Abortion Syndrome. It seemed as if my life was one continuous problem. It was one thing after another, never a moment's peace. I was a wreck!

Listen, If you are pregnant and you don't want to keep your child please consider other options before deciding to kill your baby. Abortion is not to be used as a form of birth control. It's not as easy as it sound to kill a child. You will suffer for your decision as with any other type of sin. Abortion is selfish and murder. Having a child is difficult when you're a single parent but with God my dear all things are possible.

Keith not once came to see about me or call me. The worse my life got, the worse he got. He did not care about me, or the fact that I had killed our baby. He did not want it anyway. It was not as if he was going to take care of it. I was fighting with myself and with him. I was 19 years old, by this time, not even one year after my mother's death, and I was headed down the road to death, destruction, guilt and shame.

Keith became very mean. He would start arguments with me for no apparent reason. He would break up with me to go have sex with other girls then come back to me after the one-night-stand. Sometimes he would just cheat.

He knew that he had me where he wanted me and he used that to his advantage. One night he broke up with me without giving any reason at all! I called him and he was so rude and mean. I begged him to take me back I just could not be without him. He said, "After I get some head (oral sex) from this girl I will take you back."

I said, "What!" "Are you going to give me some head?" He asked. I said, "No way!"

I know what you are thinking. He would be cut off, right? Well he was not. I loved him and even respected him for telling me the truth. At least, that is what I convinced myself that he was doing, at the time.
There would be many times that Keith would manipulate me. I was just to in love and to blind to see it.

My dad made a big issue of me always being away from home and not following his rules. He threw me out, so I moved in with Keith, his mom sister. It turned out to be the worst mistake of my life, to that point.

I did not always have the best life to begin with but moving in with Keith's family only made it worse.

There were roaches everywhere! The house was just plain nasty. I was not accustomed to living in such surroundings but somehow, I did not care. I was just happy to be with my man. I thought that since I was living with him, now, he would change and things would get better. Instead, they only got worst. Keith would leave and sometimes stay out all night.

Our fights got bigger and bigger and he would hit me or call me anything from a "bitch" to a "hoe."

After my son was born, Keith would actually have Other women come to the house. He would leave the house with them while I sat there and watched.

I could not take it anymore. I went back to my dad's house but I would still visit Keith often.

One day I went over his house so that his mom could see the baby. Keith and I were sitting on the bed and the phone rang. It was a girl he had been cheating on me with. When he got off the phone he told me that she was about to come over to bring his jacket to him. He had left it in her car. I said, "OK," and watched him walk outside. As she pulled up, he got the jacket and started a conversation with her.

Next thing I know, he jumped in the car and they pulled off. I was furious! I called his cell phone. After Keith ignored my twenty call attempts, I got her number from the caller I.D. and called it. When she answered, I asked her to put Keith on the phone. She passed the phone to him. The conversation was short. He called me a bitch and hung up on me. I could not believe it. Why was this happening to me? Why would he do some- thing so hurtful to me?

When they finally returned, hours later, I ran outside ready to fight! I asked Keith who she was. He said she was his girlfriend. You can only imagine the look on my face when he said that. I thought I was his girlfriend! Once I managed to open my mouth, I started telling the girl what was really going on. Keith went from Dr. Jekyll to Mr. Hyde instantly. He became just plain evil!

He started yelling, calling me every ugly name he could possibly think of. He started making up lies. He even told the girl I had slept with five guys at once. Then he hugged and kissed the girl, right in front of me. When I walked over to approach them, he began punching me in my head. I was totally embarrassed and hurt. I called the police. When they arrived, I told them what happened. Keith, of course, lied and told them nothing happened. They looked at my head with a flash light and could not see any wounds. Even though there were wit- nesses, they did not take him to jail. I had lost the battle all the way around. Keith laughed, got in the car with his new girlfriend and took off.

I put my son in my cousin's car forgetting all my son's things and left. I just wanted to escape and cry. When I called Keith's mother to get my son's things she was angry with me for calling the police. I could not believe her. What kind of mom gets mad at someone for calling the police on her child after he commits a crime? She put all my sons' things on the porch because she no longer wanted me in her house. I was in total disbelief. I did not know people could be so cruel and mean. All I knew is that I never wanted to hear from or see Keith again; he had done it this time!

No matter how hard I tried, however, for some reason, I just could not keep Keith off my mind. I spent the next few days in tears. I was an emotional wreck! After about three days, Keith called and apologized, as he always did. I went back, of course, as I always did. I felt I could get past his mistakes and forgive him. Little did I know I was suppressing all my hurt, pain and unforgiveness, making each time he hurt me more and more painful.

I just could not accept that Keith would remain the way he was. When I met him, he was different. I just knew there was some good on the inside of him. Soon it became very clear to me after continuing going through the same drama that Keith was not going to change.

He went back and forth with me and the other girl as much as we allowed him to. I had enough.

I began partying very hard. I decided that if Keith was going to be a jerk, so was I.

I would have my cousin take me to his house and drop my son off then we would leave. I would stay out as long as I pleased and come back when I got good-and- ready. I did not care what they thought about it. I needed my time apart from our child and I was going to get it one way or another. I became a horrible irresponsible mother. Keith's mother and sister got tired of me doing what I was doing. They never cared about what Keith was doing but when I started acting the same way, it was a problem.

They would call for me to come pick my son up and I would tell them to call Keith. I was trying to make Keith be something that he clearly had no desire to be.

After doing that for a while, Keith's mother became very frustrated. On one occasion, Keith's sister took my child to the hospital and pretended that he was sick so that I could come pick him up. After that, I quit dropping him off over there. I know I was wrong for what I was doing but back then I felt like I was right and I did not care.

In late 2004, I moved in with my friends Julie and Juwon after being put out of my grandmother's house. I was thrown out because, honestly, I was disrespectful.

At that time in my life, I was hanging with my favorite cousin. She was a very heavy weed smoker. I stayed out all night and when I did come in, I was usually so wasted that I would sleep all day. I wanted things my way and if people did not play by Christine's rules, they got no respect from me.

After moving in with my friends, I felt things were going to get better. They seemed to improve, at first. My friends got me a job and I settled right in.

Keith and I were only talking over the phone at the time. I was not too concerned about drama. After working and making a little money, I began to miss Keith I wanted him back! I know what you are thinking! "Is she crazy" YES!

Yes, I was, I began sleeping with Keith again. I knew, based upon experience that Keith and I were not going to make it so I would give my number to other people. Keith would get jealous and start fights. Sometimes, I would start the fights. I felt that he did not have a right to get upset with me, about talking to someone else, when he was doing the exact same thing.

Keith would tell me, I was the only one, he only wanted me, he needed me; all the while, he was still seeing the other girl.

One day I invited him and his cousin over for drinks. His cousin and I were very cool, at the time. We would drink and talk mess. Keith did not drink. While we were drinking, Keith started an argument. It quickly got out of hand. I ended up with a bloody nose. Juwon and his cousin, made Keith leave. Juwon told me, Keith could not come back. She did not want the drama, it could get her and the others evicted.

About 2 months later, after Keith and I had started Talking on the phone again, it seemed as if our relationship was starting to improve. I would sometimes, tell him about the other people I would talk to. I had started dating this one particular guy. Keith made me promise that I would not take Jeremiah around him but I did. I lied so that we would not have drama. I knew Keith would be upset. I did not feel that it was his place to tell me what to do but out of fear, I just wanted to keep him happy.

One day after staying the night with my male friend, Keith called and asked where I was. I was honest. I told him. He asked where Jeremiah was. I lied and told him he was with my grandmother. I told him I was on my way home and I would call him once I got there.

When I pulled up we all got out the car and went Into the house, I just happened to turn around and Keith was standing there.

He began yelling at me for having my son, with me, at

another man's house. I yelled back thinking that my male friend would step in and have my back. Keith slapped me so hard I could not see straight and my friend did nothing to protect me.

I felt so dumb and embarrassed. Once again I was let down by a man. The hurt I felt, like all the other pain, I buried deep inside and moved on.

Keith never let me forget the fact that my friend Did not have my back. He threw it in my face every chance he got. A few days, after that incident, I came home to a letter on the door, an eviction notice! The landlord happened to be a cop and had surveillance cameras set up all around the house. He saw the fight between Keith and me. He put us out.

I felt so bad. My friends had allowed me to move In with them and Keith had to come along and ruined everything. I was angry. My friends were furious.

It took us about 2 weeks to find apartment and I was determined to keep Keith far away from me. My friends also wanted me to stay away from him. I do not blame them one bit but Keith was willing to do whatever he had to do to keep me miserable.

After he got us evicted, I hated him. All the anger That I had buried inside was on its way to the surface. I was like a volcano waiting to erupt. I stayed on edge I was not a very pleasant person to be around.

Soon, Keith and I were fighting daily. I began to question our relationship. I decided it was best to move on and see other people. Little did I know, not only was Keith seeing other people, he had another baby on the way. I was crushed! I wanted to kill him, her and the baby! I was that angry!

I did not want Keith but I did not want him with anyone else. If he were to be with someone, I wanted him to be with someone who would treat him the same way he had treated me. That was not the case. He was happy and claimed to be in love.

I became very jealous. At the time, I would not Admit it. Instead, I picked fights with the girl and with Keith hoping she would get tired of the drama and leave him alone. I had turned into Keith! The fights and jealous outburst lasted a bit over a year maybe even longer.

Keith had the nerve, one day, to come over to my house and take my money because he was upset about paying child support. He hit me and ran off with my money. Naturally, I was very upset. He never gave it back.

Here I am taking care of his baby and he has the nerve to come and steal not just from me but from his own child. I was devastated. Keith treated me like I was nothing and his son did not seem to matter to him at all.

Drama, drama and more drama was the story of my life! There were many times when I would say forget it and move on to someone else just to have a little peace until one of us started another fight.
In 2005, I began dating another guy. This guy occupied all my time. Keith was the last thing on my mind. As you could imagine, Keith really did not like that.

One day, after arguing on the phone Keith came over. The argument got worse. He told me to take my clothes off. I told him, "No!" He threatened me. He told me he had a gun. I cried and cried. We went into the bedroom and I begged Him to leave me alone. He kept

Reminding me that he had a gun. I was so scared! I did not know what to think. I never saw the gun but he had his hand in his coat as if the gun were in his inside pocket. Until this day, I am not sure if he had a gun or not.

We heard a knock on the door! I told Keith that I had to answer it because it may have been one of my roommates. He followed me to the door. I opened it and ran upstairs to my neighbor's house, where my cousin was. My friends, who were at the door, came after me not knowing what was going on. All I could do was cry.

After I told them what had happen, my cousin, who was drunk at the time, went to the balcony and started yelling at Keith who, shockingly, was still down stairs. They were arguing back and forth and Keith threatened to shoot her. I kept telling her to come in and stop but she would not listen. I threatened to call the police and Keith left. Once he was gone, I called 911. They came and took my report but they did not attempt to find and arrest Keith.

After that incident, I was more terrified of Keith than ever! I stopped answering his phone calls. I did not want anything to do with him.

Meanwhile, I grew closer and closer to the other Guy. I never told him what was going on with my kid's Dad. I did not want to scare him away.

Somewhere around July of that same year, I found Myself pregnant with the new guy's baby. A part of me was excited and a part of me just felt horrible and nasty. "Look at me two babies with two different baby daddies," I thought.

My excitement came from thinking that if I have this man's baby Keith was sure to leave me alone but after thinking about it a little more, I decided I did not want the baby. I began drinking, smoking and punching myself in my stomach. I had no money for an abortion and I was not ready for another baby.

My self-destructive behavior paid off. I rushed to the bathroom after feeling moisture. I was bleeding. I went to the hospital and sure enough, I had miscarried.

I know it sounds bad but I was so happy that I Was no longer pregnant. I told myself, from that point on, I was going to do better and for a few months, I did.

Keith was back in my life. He and I were not Communicating on a regular basis but were cordial. We eventually, decided to hook up and go to the birthday party given for one of his friends.

I remember the exact date. It was November 3, 2005. There was liquor and food and I got wasted.

After the party, we went back to Keith's house; as You can imagine, I had sex with him. Once I woke up, I knew I had made a mistake. I remember praying, "Lord please don't let me get pregnant!"
I could not get another abortion the next one would kill me. I did not want another baby by Keith.

I left it alone and went on about my life. On December 20, that same year, my twenty-first birthday I became very sick. In fact, I was so sick I could not get drunk. I just remember laying on the floor barely conscious, seeing Keith and My friend Julie walk in from the store. They asked what was wrong and I did not know. I

Went to the hospital and for the fourth time I was pregnant!

I was so angry with myself. I thought to myself, "I got drunk and smoked with the last baby and killed it. I can do it again." I looked up on the internet how to kill your baby with over the counter products. I found that vinegar and castor oil would get the job done. I chose castor oil because vinegar could kill me; at least that is what it said.

I went to my local pharmacy, picked up what I Needed and drank away. The only result was nonstop bowl movements. Keith, in the meantime, was still the same old Keith, mean, arrogant, a liar, cheater, horrible father and abusive in every way. I could not bear to have another kid by him. I asked Keith if he could get the money for another abortion. He told me, "Yes." I was excited. I never thought about the fact that I was killing a person, or that God may have a plan for my baby's life. I just did not care.

Keith failed to come through with the money, Leaving me no choice but to have the baby. I started the pregnancy by not eating right and smoking cigarettes because I wanted the baby to die. Every time I went to the doctor, I wanted them to tell me my baby was not going to make it or that it was already dead. Instead, they told me how healthy my baby was and how perfect my child was going to be.

After a few months, I began to fall in love with my unborn child and accepted that I would once again give birth. It was the same old thing with Keith. He never

Showed up at any doctor's appointments. He made no effort to see how the baby and I were doing. While this was going on, Keith, once again, got another girl pregnant. Our due dates were only two or three months apart.

The only time Keith acted concerned about the baby was when he caught me smoking. He would get upset and yell or snatch the cigarette from me. I hated it. I knew smoking was not healthy for my child or me but I felt I needed to smoke because I was under so much stress. It seemed to calm me down.

I went through another nine months alone with no Support from Keith. My baby girl, Khrystiana, was born July 30, 2006.

The day I went into labor Keith was with his other Baby mama, so he showed up at the hospital late. My family was not pleased with Keith's behavior and they told him so. When he responded, an argument got started, right there in the hospital. Yup, they were arguing while I lay there with my new baby girl and a sore body. I really did not care; I guess I had grown immune to his mess. His foolishness no longer fazed me. I allowed Keith to hold his baby and did not say a word.

I was not home a good week before I received a Call telling me to rush my child to Children's Hospital, in Detroit.

I asked what was wrong, they said something was wrong with her blood I went into full panic mode. Once at the hospital they told us there were elevated levels of something in her blood. I had no idea what they were talking about. Until this day, I have no idea. All I knew

Was my baby was sick! They told me the condition could be deadly.

I began to pray. Even though I hated God, I always knew he did not hate me. I called everyone I knew who could pray, the doctors were constantly poking at my baby with needles and she was grumpy because she could not eat.

I was miserable. Do you think Keith showed up? No! He did not! He had every excuse in the book so I had to go through this with my aunt. Even though she was there, I still felt alone. I spent the night at the hospital worried about my baby and praying.

The next day the doctors came to me and said that My baby was normal. He said he could not explain it. He knew she was sick and had test to prove it but now she was perfectly fine. I took my baby home that day! My heart really began to soften towards God.

About two weeks later, I was back in the streets clubbing and having fun. The physical fighting between Keith and I had slowed down a lot. We argued a lot but there was a lot less pushing, shoving and hitting.

He never showed any interest in his children. Eventually his lack of concern began to anger me.
I moved back in with Him but things were not different. He was still a liar and a cheat.

One night, while I was at a friend's house drinking, he told me he was coming to get the kids. He never showed up so I found a sitter and my friend, my cousin and I went out looking for him. We drove all around Pontiac until I saw the car. We parked and waited for Keith to come out. I called his phone but got no answer.

After sitting for a while, we left. The next day when Keith got home, I asked him where he was. He told me his sister's house. Granted his sister did stay on the same street and since I had never been over to her house I had to take his word.

I acted as if everything was fine but I knew some-Thing was not right and I was determined to find out what it was. Luckily, Keith ended up leaving and his sister showed up. I sparked a conversation and then asked her was Keith at her house last night. She said what I had expected her to say, "No!"

After finding out whom he was with I called the Girl in an attempt to tell her everything that was going On. Keith was with her at the time. Naturally, he called me a liar and all sorts of other names. When he came home, he put me out, leaving my babies and me without a place to go.

He told the girl and a few other people that I had HIV! I could not believe he was doing that to me especially after all we had gone through. I could not help but think why me!

I kept going back to him. Each time I did, I hated myself, the more I cried, the more I wanted to die and the more I thought about suicide.

Around 2007, Keith and I really began to fall apart. I was drinking all the time with his sisters and my friends. Keith would be gone to only God knows where. It was a horrible relationship.

We both began to work at the same job and Keith began being very distant, I Knew what that meant. Keith had another girl on the side. We argued until I could not

Argue anymore! I would wait on him to come over after he told me he would. He would never show up I got tired of him and his mess. I promised myself not to have sex with him again. I was tired of being used for my body and I did not want to catch an STD!

I also went back to church and gave my life back To the Lord. I wanted to stop running and do what was right. I was baptized and filled with the Holy Ghost at the end of 2007. I had quit drinking and smoking everything was good. My boss liked me so he would give me double the money on my checks.

I joined the choir at church and was doing one of The things I knew God had called me to do which was to Sing. I felt like everything was going to get better from there.

When Keith would call and want to fight, I would just ignore him. There was a change in me.

One day I went to cash my check and the guy I dated in 2005, happened to be there. I must say I was so excited. We exchanged numbers and immediately picked up where we left off in spite of my newfound salvation. Against my better judgment, I began sleeping with the guy. Keith was, once again, on the back part of my brain. I wanted nothing to do with him.

A few months into me dating this other guy Keith starts, of course, being jealous again. He did not even want me back he just wanted to have sex with me so he could feel like he had control. I was not having it I ignored Keith I would not give him the time of day. That is when the madness began all over again.

Keith came to me acting as if he really loved me and he wanted to be saved and do what is right. He did not want to lose me. I fell for it all!

I took Keith back and let the other guy go. Keith Came to church with me every Sunday and things were actually going well. We even got engaged! I was so excited I just knew that God had turned it all around and Keith and I would live happily ever after. How wrong I was!

I found out that Keith was still messing with some Girl he met when we were working together. Instead of breaking it off, however, I decided I would get even.

One night I went out with my cousin and I met a Guy and gave him my number. Keith was at my house at the time watching the kids. When I got home, my phone rang. The caller I.D. read, "Private." At first, I thought it might be Keith or one of the girls he was sleeping with calling to play on the phone and harass me, as they often did. I answered. It was the new guy I had met.

I was drunk. I started talking to the guy on the phone not thinking about the fact that Keith was in the house. My cousin reminded me so I lowered my voice.

When I got off the phone, I went upstairs where Keith was. He started questioning me and of course, I Lied. He asked who was I talking to and what had I done at the club. I just wanted him to leave me alone so I could go to bed. Suddenly, He jumped on top of me and began choking me I was shocked! He had never done that before. I could not get him off me! I could barely breath, but I managed to say, "Keith what about the kids?" He stopped and got off of me.

I cried all night Keith apologized but I did not want to hear it. I just wanted to end it. The next day, before church, I told my pastor and he was not pleased. Keith went to talk to him after I did and my pastor told him about his deplorable behavior.

During service, I cried and cried. I was so miserable. People were asking me what was wrong. I acted as if everything was fine. I told them I was tired. When I went up for prayer a girl prophesied to me that Keith and I were meant to be. I knew that she had missed it there was no way that God was going to allow me to stay with that crazy man.

After that service, I told Keith I was done. I could Not do it anymore. This time, I was serious. He acted as if he did not care.

I stopped seeing Keith and went back to the other guy. I did not know what Keith was up to and I did not care. I was finally rid of him. Though I was wavering, I was still in the church.

Chapter 4
The Rape

One day my phone rang. The caller I.D. revealed it was Keith. I would not answer. I did not want to talk to him. On top of that, I was waiting for my new guy to call and come over.

Keith must have called at least six times; back-to-back. I still refused to answer. Suddenly, I heard someone banging on my door as if he had lost his mind.

At the time, Keith's cousin and her boyfriend were in the house with me. I told them not to answer the door. I knew it was Keith and I hoped he would just go away. He did not. Instead, he kicked my door in just as he had done before. He ran upstairs, to the second floor of the house and grabbed me. I told him to let me go or I was to call the police. He let me go and the yelling, screaming, and arguing back and forth began. The argument was about nothing. Keith just felt that I should do whatever he told me to do without question and I just did not want to do that anymore.

He grabbed me again. I pulled away and called the police. Keith began to make threats. The threats scared me so much that I called them back to tell them not to come. Secretly, I was hoping they would realize I was in trouble and come anyway. They never showed up! For those who may be asking, did his cousin or her boyfriend help, me the answer is NO!

Keith left and I sat on my couch and cried my eyes Out. My male friend came over and sat with me. I told him what happened. He did not understand why I

Would put up with such crap. He did not make me feel any better. He did not understand. *Just as many of you do not understand why a woman would stay in an abusive relationship. Never make a battered woman feel anymore unsafe than she already feels. Being there for her that is the best thing you can do.*

I asked him to leave. I just wanted to be by myself. I was accustomed to the lonely feeling. I had gone through so much. I felt I had no one I could turn to.

A few days had passed and I was over Keith's Aunt's house. I loved to be around her. She seemed to have so much insight. I felt I could talk to her about anything. While there, my friend called and wanted me to be dropped off at his place. I asked Keith's aunt and she agreed to take me. I was so excited.

As I waited for her to get ready, Keith popped up. I spoke to him and went outside. After a few minutes, he followed and started arguing with me.

He swore up and down I was trying to play him. "You trying to get my aunt to drop you off to that niggas house," he grumbled. I was shocked! In that moment I felt so betrayed and hurt but then I began thinking, "No she would not do that to me, she just wouldn't!

Keith's aunt ran out the house to calm Keith Down. She told his cousin and me to get into the car. Keith jumped in right behind us. In fact, he jumped right into my lap. He grabbed me by my neck and began choking me. I thought he was going to kill me. I could not get him off no matter how hard I tried.

His cousin and aunt both tried to help but they Could not get him off either.

My eyes felt like they were about to pop out of my head and I could hardly breathe. All I could think about was my already deceased mother, my siblings and my children. I was surely about to die, Keith's aunt told him to get off me or she would call the police and he jumped up. As soon as Keith was out of the car, we locked the doors and his aunt took me to the police station.

I had my male friend and my dad meet me there. My father insisted that I go home with him but I refused. I would much rather go with my friend and get drunk. After that episode, I ignored all Keith's calls. I wanted nothing to do with him and I made sure I was never alone.

About a week had passed and Keith began to send messages about how sorry he was. He even went over to my dad's house to apologize to him.

That really angered me. If I were my father I Would had beat the crap out of Keith. Not my dad; he is a peacemaker. Keith made a promise to my dad never to lay another hand on me again.

The following weekend, Keith asked if I needed Any money for our son's school. I of courses said, "Yes," after all he never offered, so I had better take it while I can.

He came over to give me the money. I remember the exact date. It was Monday, September 15. I was sitting talking to my sister as she washed clothes at my house. I remember being very rude to Keith. I just hated him! I wanted him to feel the same way he made me feel. He was really trying to get me back so I used that to my advantage.

He then pulled me aside and asked if I would have sex with him. When I said, "No," he offered me to give me $50 if I would change my mind and sleep with him. I told him, "No," again and laughed it off. I told him he was crazy.

I could tell by the look on his face, he did not like My response. He took the money he had given me for our son and left.

I laughed as I told my sister about it and went on about my day.

Around 9:00 that evening, my sister left. About that time, Keith called. He asked if I still wanted the money for our son's school. I told him yes, if he wanted to give it to me. He said, "Okay," and asked if I would ride to the store with him so he could get some change. I agreed. I got the kids together. When Keith pulled up, we left.

We drove to his mom's house. I asked why we were there. He said he had to get his name brand glasses. He was going to sell them to one of his friends. He suggested we leave the children with his mom while we went to meet his friend.

In my mind that was fine. It made sense. I was actually happy. The kids could stay with Keith's mom while I go on my date with my friend.

Keith and I went to the store to get change. He Gave me $30. I did not complain. I was happy to get something, anything.

He then took me home and asked if he could come in to get his friends clothes. His friend had stayed the

Night with Keith a while back. I told him that was fine. I then went upstairs leaving Keith alone downstairs.

Keith came upstairs to my bedroom where I stood by the door. Again, He asked if I we could have sex. Again, I told him no.

He turned the lights of and said, "Well, we are any Way!
"   I chuckled, thinking, this was just another one of Keith's crazy spells. As usual, we would fight and he would leave. Unfortunately, this time, I was wrong.

He told me to take my clothes off; "are you serious?" I asked, sarcastically. He was serious!

He lifted up his shirt and I saw my kitchen butcher knife tucked in his pants. I knew then he was not playing! I began to cry and beg him not to do that to me. Keith was not hearing it. It was as if he had stepped out- side himself and let the devil take complete control. All the anger, all the stress he may have had was about to explode in my direction.

He yelled at me, calling me every name in the book! He hit me. When I thought it could not get any worse, when I thought Keith would not do anything as harsh as taking something from me that I could never get back. He raped me! I cried and cried! I just wanted him to get off me and go away.

I felt nasty, violated, sick, ugly, unwanted, unworthy, guilty, and ashamed; like thrown away trash. His touch was not loving, but hard and violent. It was obvious that he meant to hurt me and he did just that.

After he was done, I rushed to put my panties Back on. Keith told me to lie down. I kept looking out of

The window. Keith would tell me I had better not scream or he would hurt me so I kept quiet even though I wanted to scream for help. I had no choice but to keep my mouth closed.

Keith lay in the bed next to me, yelling at me about the other guy; as if I owed him something. I began telling Keith that I loved him and that I needed him; any- thing to keep him calm.

He told me I was lying, jumped on me and choked me. I thought to myself, "This is my day. September 15, 2008, I am going to die!"

There was no one there to get Keith off me and I Had no strength to get him off myself. I knew I was not Going to make it. He choked me. I could not speak aloud but in my mind, I called on Jesus. I really believe it was God who gave me the strength to push my legs up and push Keith off me. The knife, he had placed back in the top of his boxers, cut him on his abdomen. It made him even angrier.

I asked if he was ok though I really did not care. I just wanted to try to keep him calm but he just kept raging.

I asked him could I smoke a cigarette. Angrily, he Said, "Yes." I did not have a lighter so I had to go down-Stairs to use the stove. Keith held my hand to make sure that I would not try to get away. I felt as if I had been kidnapped and held hostage in my own home. Come to think of it I was!

After smoking Keith saw fit to rape me 2 more times each time he thrust into me, I felt a piece of me leave! At the time, I did not understand what I was feeling. I did not get why I felt so dead; so vulgar. I just knew that something had been stolen from me; something I could never get back.

After being tortured for hours; yes, rape is torture! I had to think of how I would get away. Not only get away but also how could I get away without dying or getting beat up.

I told Keith that I had to go to the Work First proGram in the morning and asked would he take me. He agreed after telling me I had better not tell anyone he had raped me. The reason I said the Work First program is because I knew that Keith was aware of the program. I figured He would probably believe I would have to get up as early as seven o'clock, to get there on time.

I lay there all night trying my best not to fall Asleep. I set my alarm for seven. When it went off, I jumped out the bed and ran to the bathroom. I leaned against the wall and silently cried as I ran the shower.

I had no intention of getting into the shower. I was Going to the police and I did not want to wash away the evidence. As the shower ran, I put on my clothes and made sure to look as new and clean as possible because I did not want Keith to suspect anything.

After coming out the bathroom, I asked Keith Could I have my phone. He had been holding it all night. He gave it to me and went to move his car; it had been parked in the front of my apartment building all night.

Once he walked out of the door, I called my sister And told her that Keith had been raping me all night. The phone hung up mid call so I called again. She heard me and said she was on her way.

Keith came in as I was putting the phone into my pocket. He grabbed me and told me not to tell. I promised I would not.

My sister pulled up and I ran outside, forgetting to Close and lock my door. I did not care. We then took my sister's boyfriend who was Keith's brother who was with her home and went straight to the police station from there.

Once at the police station I went to the window and said in a very timid voice, "I need to make a police report. I have been raped." They gave me the paper work to fill out but I could not write. I was shaken! I started crying again and I could not stop. At times, I would almost go into a state of panic.

A female sergeant came into the room and asked Me to come with her. We went into a room in the back of the police station so I could have some privacy. I broke down again, crying hysterically!

As I was telling her what happened. Keith sent a Text message to my phone saying, he was going to kill himself. I really did not care whether he did or he did not. I showed the message to the officer and she documented it. She then told me to tell her, in detail, what had happened. I could not simply say, "He raped me three times." She wanted a blow-by-blow description of the entire horrible evening. I had to say, "He put his penis inside of me and begin to pump very hard."

It was very uncomfortable for me. I felt so embarrassed, ashamed and humiliated a small part of me just wanted to get up and walk away.

After telling my story, I broke down again. I told the sergeant about all the times I had called the police and nothing was done. I told her the next thing worst to rape is death and I did not want to die.

She looked at me and said, "Christine, I promise you I am going to get him. Do not worry about it. You are safe now." As much as I wanted to believe her, I just could not. I had been let down so many times before. I trusted no one.

The police officers arranged for me to go to the Rape victim's clinic. My dad went with me. Police officers followed in another vehicle.

Once there, I could not stop crying. The whole Thing was so surreal. I just could not believe it! The nurse came in and again I had to tell my story. I really did not want to go through the whole thing again but knew I had to. Once again, the feeling of shame and embarrassment came over me. After telling her what happened she took me into an examination room.

I had to take all my clothes off. Still traumatized, from the assault, the examination made me feel violated again. I wish I knew how to put into words exactly how I felt but the truth of the matter is I simply cannot. I did not want anyone touching me or looking at me. I was used goods, unworthy of any love, compassion or any kind of intimacy.

The nurse touched me on every part of my body, as she felt for bruises. She took hair samples from my head and my vagina, to see if Keith's had left any DNA behind. I felt, violated, like a piece of rotten meat. I cried, and cried and cried some more.

My dad and step mom were there but I wanted my mother. I needed her. Here I am, twenty-three years old at a rape clinic, experiencing every woman's nightmare and my mother was gone. I was more than miserable.

Once the nurse was done with the examination, I Was finally able to take a shower. I was so excited! That was the best part of the day for me. I had walked around all day with Keith's sperm leaking from my body. I felt disgusting.

After leaving the clinic, I went home to meet the police so they could collect more evidence. When the police were done at the apartment, I headed straight to Keith's aunt's house.

When I got there, Keith's family members were Anxious to hear what had happened. I told them and they acted as if they were on my side. I was so happy because I did not want anyone to be angry at me for doing what I knew was right. Keith had certainly crossed the line and he needed to pay for what he had done.

After being at his aunt's for a few hours, I decided I would go to Bible Study. I needed to talk to my pastor. He was the only one I felt would understand and the only one I felt I could trust. I told him everything that happened. I told him I was going to go home and get drunk. He told me not to but I did not know what else to do. Praying was not an option because, once again, I felt let down by God. Why would he allow me to go through such a horrible ordeal? I felt like God hated me. I did not understand why my life had spiraled out of control. I was eighteen, minding my own business and then my mother passed away. After that, everything fell apart. What did I do?

I went home that night with a fifth of gin. I sat there with one of Keith's cousins and drank until I was numb. I did not know how to process what I was feeling. I did not want to deal with it. I sat up talking to Keith's cousin about how I was feeling. She showed so much concern, I was so happy. She was there, by my side.

That night I could not sleep even after consuming All that liquor! It was as if a dark cloud of fear had come over me. I felt so afraid.

The next day I asked my cousin if I could stay With her. I did not want to be at home. I was afraid to be alone. She said, "Yes." For a week, I stayed at her house. I felt safe there because no one knew where I was. I felt that people would taunt me even though, so far, nothing like that had happened.

_____Chapter 5_____
Trusting the Wrong People

    I guess you are wondering where my male friend was during this horrible time. Well, let me tell you. I called him after I left the police station and told him what had happened. He hung up in my face. Yes! He did! I did not hear from him again until a week later. He told me he was scared because people get killed in those types of situations. Yes! He did! No, I did not break it off with him. Instead, I embraced him more than ever because I felt I needed him. I know, I know, crazy right? From that day on, he was right there.

    That same week I got a phone call telling me not to Show up in court. I began getting rude, threatening text messages. One day my sister and I went to the mall. As we were walking in, three girls were walking out. When they saw me, they turned around, came in and began following my sister and me.

    They did not say anything they just followed us Closely. In that moment, I went from fear to anger to insaine!

    By the time they stopped following us and went on their way, I was so infuriated I could hardly breathe. My sister tried her best to calm me down but it did not work. We ended up leaving the mall before we finished shopping.

    The next day I went to a clothing store with my best friend. The same girls were there. I heard one of them say, "That's her." I began walking in her direction. I was ready to fight.

My friend grabbed me and we left. I could not believe it. Here I am a victim of a crime and I am being treated as if I am the one who raped someone.

As the weeks went on people would come up to me; people that I did not know, they would ask me what happened. Some would come up to me and tell me all types of untrue things they heard. It was ridiculous. I was so angry and so hurt I wanted to die! I was the talk of the town. All of Pontiac was buzzing about me. It was the kind of attention that I did not want.

My sister was still dating Keith's brother. Their relationship was rocky but they had a baby to take care of. They were trying to make the best of it.

My sister was totally stressed. Keith's family had turned on me. They believed the lies Keith told them. Be-because she was dating his brother, she felt as if she was caught in the middle.

Keith's cousin was still cool with me even though my dad and my other family members and friends told me not to trust her. I did so, in spite of their warnings. She and my sister would come back and tell me things that Keith's family was saying about me. I would just cry. They called me a liar. It made me feel raped all over again.

When I found out that Keith's aunt was one of the ones talking about me I was crushed. I had grown to love and trust her. I felt like such an idiot but as the saying goes, blood is thicker than water. I felt like I was going to have a nervous breakdown. I would literally sit down and rock back and forth. I felt crazy my life was headed

Down the wrong path. One more hurt or pain and I was not going to make it.

   The first court date came and all of Keith's family was there. My family was there also, so was my pastor and my male friend. It was just an arraignment so nothing really happened but the setting of the date I would testify. After court, my father was angry with me for having my male friend there. He said it would just cause drama. Looking back, I can see my father's point. However, at that time I did not want to hear that. Why should I care how they feel when a member of their family had just done the unthinkable to me? I honestly did not ask him to come to make anyone upset. He came to support me. Later on, I did find out that the family was angry. They felt it was a slap in Keith's face.

   I did not care what they thought. Why in the world would they be more focused on who was at the court than the fact that a member of their family was facing almost sixty years in prison is beyond me. It was not there business and that was not the issue. I felt it was immature, petty and just darn right stupid.
   After finding out they were angry about my friend being there, I knew they were just digging for something they could use to stir up drama. I was not about to give them the satisfaction so I left it alone and went on about my business.
   After about a month later, it was time for the second Court date after about 20 outfit changes I was finally ready to go.

When we arrived at court, I broke down in the room. I was not ready to see Keith. My dad, step mom and the prosecutor calmed me down and prepared me for one of the scariest moments of my life. I pulled myself together, held my head up and went into the courtroom. My family sat to the right of me and his family sat in front of me and so did he. I wanted to run out the courtroom. I felt so intimidated and nauseous but I could not show it. I sat in that chair and I told what happened exactly the way it happened.

I tried not to cry but when the prosecutor asked how it made me feel when he was raping me, I could not control my emotions. That was the first time I was able to say how it made me feel out loud, in front of Keith. Keith looked at me with no remorse. I wanted to jump over the stand and kick him in the face. The more I sat there giving my testimony the more comfortable I got and I just remember staring Keith right in his eyes and him turning away. He could not even look at me. I did not just hate what Keith had done to me; I hated him. To make matters worse, Keith tells his attorney that I only accused him of rape because I was angry that he had someone else pregnant. I had no idea anyone was pregnant. I was shocked!

There were two girls sitting on my family's side that I did not know. One of them was the girl Keith had been sleeping with. I did not care. I just wanted him to pay for what he had done to me.

When court was over, that day, I could not wait to go home so I could get drunk and smoke a cigarette. I spent my days at home drinking so I would not feel the

Pain. I spent many nights at the club so I could forget what happened. I wanted to have fun. I did not want to deal with the pain. It was so much easier to run from it.

Keith's family members hung out at the same club. I would act as if they were not there. I was out to have fun and forget they existed. Soon they began using the fact that I was at the club as a way to say I had not been raped. If I had been raped, why would I be out at the club drinking? I was so angry. I felt they were all hypocrites. Half of them were alcoholics though they would never admit it. I had heard the stories about how some of them had also been molested and raped. How dare they say anything about me.

I was so angry. I wanted them to shut up and leave me alone. I was not bothering anyone so why would anyone bother me.

The next week when I went to the club Keith's sister made sure I did not have any fun. Whenever I got out on the dance floor, she would get up and get up close to me. She would flail her arms wildly as she danced. I knew she was doing it on purpose. I was determined not to let her run me away.

After a while, she and another girl began following me around. Everywhere I looked, they were there. I Told my cousin and my brother what was going on. They told me not to worry, just do not go anywhere alone.

I sat down with my brother because honestly I just wanted to cry and go home. I did not get why they were doing that to me. The next thing I know, as I was talking to my brother they came and sat at a nearby table. They

Leaned back, trying to hear what I was saying. That was it for me. I wanted to go home so I left.

They got just what they wanted and I was not going to go back again. I hated my life and I did not care anymore.

I called a girl from my church because I needed to Talk to someone. I wanted to live a responsible Christian life but I could not help but think I was not worthy. I had done too much and gone too far. She told me to call her husband because he would understand. I did and not long after, a rumor started. People were saying I wanted her husband. I must say I felt betrayed and hurt. I do not know who started the rumor and I really did not care. All I knew is that it was not true and it hurt.

I was already feeling alone and if I cannot trust my Brothers and sisters in Christ then, who can I trust. I no longer wanted to attend church and I was determined to stay away from it but something just would not allow me to go that far.

As time went on, I got a job at a small manufacturing plant. One of Keith's sisters worked there so I knew t I probably would not be there long. I was excited to have a job. Christmas was coming and I needed a car. I made some new friends and I was finally happy.

One day, while at work, after only being there for about a month, I happened to be talking to a co-worker about some of the things that were going on in my life. She shared some of what she was going through as well. Keith's sister walked by; she did not look too pleased. The next thing I know, they called everyone in the department into a meeting. Our supervisor asked was anyone sending out threats I looked around, as did everyone else. No one said anything so the meeting ended as suddenly as it had been called.

As I was leaving, the supervisor called me to her Office and fired me. When I asked why she said I had been making threats against Keith's sister. She would not allow me to explain. She had no interest my side of the story. As you can imagine, I was angry. Violent thoughts went through my head. I wanted to kill her! I was already going through enough with the rape case, taking care of two kids, being taunted by Keith's other friends and family members and now this. Now she gets me fired!

Secretly, I plotted to get revenge. I did not know how. I did not know when but the day would surly come. I would pay her back for what she had done.

I had written down a whole budget plan to get my Car, my kids Christmas gifts and pay bills. Now it was ruined, because of one person's hatred towards me.

I left the job with my head held high because I did not want anyone to see me cry. Once my ride came, I broke down. I was already miserable. Having a job and being able to provide and get the things needed for me, the kids and my household was the only thing I had to hold on to.

I was in counseling at the time with Haven, a women's shelter and advocacy group. I told my counselor everything that happened. She set me up with a church that would help me out with gifts for the kids for Christmas. Christmas was only about two weeks away I was grateful that she helped me. I still did not think that a church function would be enough to give my babies a good Christmas. I went to the event and I must say I was blown away! They gave me two large black garbage bags and allowed me 30 minutes to walk through this large room full of brand new toys, coats and shoes to get all that I could. It was the best Christmas ever for the kids.

That Christmas Eve night my cousin, Crystal, called me. She told me that my aunt, Francis, was in the hospital and that she probably was not going to make it. The next morning, Christmas day, my aunt died. I was very sad, you see my aunt stayed with us before my mother passed and she would watch us all the time when we were younger. She was very humorous and I loved to be around her. Aunt Francis was a God fearing woman and she did not play about her daughter, Crystal, or my little cousins. It makes me laugh talking about it because when we would mess with one of our cousins Aunt Francis eyes would get big and she would throw a house shoe at us or say, "Get on here!" Another thing about my aunt that I always admired was the fact that just like my mother she was real!

She was not the type to put on a show. She spoke The truth and she did not care what people said. When she came to me and said she knew my cousin had molested me I knew she knew more, of course, at the time she could not tell me but I knew we were on the same page. Until this day, I would like to find out how the molestation cycle started.

It's a fact that molestation is a learned behavior. People don't wake up one day wanting to molest. They repeat what has been done to them or have seen done to someone else.

Aunt Francis is truly missed she will always hold A special place in my heart. I loved her dearly and I know without a shadow of doubt that she loved me.

As time passed into the New Year, I was still fighting my rape case. It was a long, frustrating, nerve racking process. It was now time for trial. I went prepared to fight. When I arrived at the courthouse, my lawyer came to me and asked if I would agree to a plea deal.

Keith would get one year for felonious assault with a deadly weapon. When I asked why, she said it was because our evidence was circumstantial. It may not hold up at trial. She said I could take the deal or Keith could possibly get out that day. Afraid that we could lose, I accepted the plea. I sat out in the hall waiting while the attorneys talked. Keith's family and friends walked past and rolled their eyes in a most evil way.

Once the hall was clear, my attorney asked how I Was feeling. I immediately began to cry and scream. I was furious. Here I am the victim of a horrific crime and Keith is getting a break. His family is looking at me as if I had raped him! My godmother talked to me and calmed me down. She kept telling me that it was not over. As much as I wanted to believe her I just could not help but think, "This man held me against my will for ten hours; raped and abused me and he was only about to receive one year. I was the victim and I would suffer far longer than that."

I was already suffering. My lawyer kept asking Me did I feel like she had talked me into accepting the plea. I never answered because honestly, I did feel that way. I was so angry and disappointed that I wanted to pick her up and throw her out of the window.

I wanted my mother that day. I went all the way back to being that teen-aged girl again. I wanted nothing else but to see Donna Marie Gulley walk through those court doors.

It's funny how when you are upset about one thing, everything else that you're upset about comes up as well.

At that moment, abandonment set in. I was devastated! Even now, I see a vision of me sitting in that hall- way, looking down the hall into a dark hole. That folks; is how it felt. I felt dead; like I had lost everything and once again, God did not fight for me. Keith had won and I, the victim, had lost.

Chapter 6
What Was I Thinking?

Two weeks, after I reluctantly agreed to the plea deal, we went back to court for the sentencing. I made sure my hair was done, my make-up was laid and my outfit was new. I was determined not to look as bad as I felt. I went into the courtroom, sat down the chair beside the prosecutor and prepared to read my statement. No matter what, I was going to stand strong.

Keith's whole family came. I only had about four people there to support me. No one knew what I was going through. For some odd reason, my father did not want anyone else in our family to know. The ones that did know had to work or go to school so they could not be there.

Keith's family sat to the left of me whispering and looking at me. I guess they were trying to intimidate me. His girlfriend did the same.

I sat patiently waiting my turn. Keith went before Me and I must say my heart went out to him because he Looked sick. He looked as if he had not eaten for weeks. His hair was a mess. For some reason I had a bit of compassion for him.

Keith apologized. His apology made me furious Because I knew that he did not mean it. He would not even admit to what he had done. He tried to make me look like the one in the wrong.

When Keith apologized, his family got loud in the Courtroom; they called me a bitch among other things

The guards did nothing to shut them up. I could not believe it; they just stood there watching in silence.

Now it was my turn I got up and told exactly how I felt. All the while, I could hear Keith's family, in the background, making rude, ugly comments.

I made it clear that no one knew what happened But Keith, God and me, when I said that; they became even more upset.

They just knew they had it figured out. The way they saw it, I was jealous because Keith had some other girl pregnant so I made up a lie to get back at him.

When I was finished speaking, a police officer escorted my family and I out the courtroom. Once we were in the car Keith's girlfriend called my sister and me and began yelling into her cell phone calling us a Bitches I got a little upset but not much. I knew the day would come when I would run into her under different circumstances and it was going to go down.

I was at the top of feeling defeated. I had lost. I Was twenty-four years old and I had been losing since I was eighteen. I decided if you cannot beat them join them. I was going to live my life the way I pleased. No one was going to tell me anything! I was already drinking like crazy and it was about to get worse. I stayed at the clubs and all the other hang out spots. If there was no party at the clubs, I brought one to my house.

I would get so drunk I could not remember my own name. I started hanging, with Keith's sister, hard. We will call her Kendra. She became my best friend in spite of what had happened between her brother and me.

Before the rape and throughout the rape Kendra stuck by my side. We were very close. She had my back and even though she was bigger, I had hers too. She was a part of a group called U.S., meaning, "Usual Suspects." These guys were awesome, I had met them long before 2009 but because I was with Keith all the time, I could never associate with them. He was so jealous he did not want me to have many friends.

This time around, Kendra had her own house and we were partying every single night. I would be wasted dancing all around the house and just having a good time.

Around this time, Keith's other sister, Martha, and I had rekindled our relationship, as well. To my surprise, a few weeks later, another of Keith's sisters, we will call her Tonya, the one who got me fired, was also ready to let go of some things.

We would all get together and get wasted. I had even talked to Keith on the phone. I was looking forward to his release in July. What! I know that is your reaction! I figured; if you could not beat them join them. After all, I had lost any way!

I ended up sleeping with one of the guys in the Group. That opened the door for many more. Once I let The cat out of the bag, I was not putting it back in. I wanted liquor and men wanted sex. By the time, July came around and Keith was released. I had already slept with nine other men.

Another reason for my promiscuity was the fact that I had been raped and nothing, serious, had been done about it. I figured If I gave it up I would never

Have to worry about another rape. All I wanted was liquor, cigarettes and maybe some food or a few dollars cash.

I know some of you reading this are like, "What was she thinking?" You have not heard anything yet. When Keith got out whom do you think he came home to? I can see you now! Not you! Christine please do not say he came home to you! Yes! He did. I slept with him and everything. Can you believe that? Yes I did!

Listen… when you feel like everything that can be done to you has been done to you and the only thing left is murder you will do anything. If sleeping with Keith would keep him on my side; that is what I was going to do. The only thing worse than rape, is killing someone and I did not want to die.

Keith's family, of course, and my family thought I Had lost my mind. I do not blame them. I just did not know how to explain to them why I was doing what I was doing. Heck, I would not be able to explain why I did what I did to you, if I had not found myself through the power of Jesus and some help from counselors.

That night, before I slept with him, he apologized For everything he had done.

I thought I had let it go. He then brought up all the Men I slept with and all the partying I had been doing. Now you tell me how a man who has been gone a year knows all that information. The cousin, that I had grown suspicious about that was living with me, had been telling Keith and her family all my business. Keith knew detail for detail. She was not my friend she was a snake the whole time!

I admitted that everything that he said was true. I could tell that there was something different about Keith and I took full advantage of it.

I had changed so much after the rape. I became More aggressive, bold, bitter and angry. I was the wrong one to play with before, when it came to females. Now I was just the wrong one period. I did not care if you were a bear; you were going down.

I let Keith know that and he knew that I was serious. He had known me for a long time and had heard the things that he was now hearing about me. He had never seen me act in such violent ways. He knew that what he had done had changed me.

I slept with Keith, off and on, for about one month. In spite of the occasional sex, we both knew that a serious relationship was not going to happen. There was simply too much bad history. Keith was still involved with the girl he had got pregnant before he went to jail. Besides, I began coming to my senses. I was sleeping with the same guy that had raped me!

Not long after our last sexual encounter in July the girl Keith had been messing with began to text my phone. She would send messages talking about my kids; she was calling them all types of names. I let it go because I called my pastor and told him about it. He told me not to do anything. I was mad at Keith for continuing to mess with a woman who was dogging his children. He swore up and down he was done with her. He was not going to allow anyone to disrespect his kids. I knew he was a bald-faced liar so I took matters into my own hands. I could not take it anymore. I found out where the girl stayed, drove over there and parked my truck right next to Keith's car. I called his phone since he claimed not to be spending time around her, to let him know that I was outside. He laughed and said, "No you ain't." I said, Ok come on out. He came outside and could not believe his eyes. I was right where I said I would be. I told him to tell her to come outside so I could beat her up. He refused so I left. That night she continued to play on my phone so I called in to work picked up my cousins and went on a mission.

 I went to the club where she was. There were too many people with her for only three of us to take so we left and waited in my truck. Keith was with her too but I did not care. I wanted to hurt her.

 When the club closed for the night, Keith, the girl and one of his sisters got into their car and they left. I followed close behind I ran red lights and stop signs. I was not about to lose them.

 We ended up right back at the girl's house and I was ready. I jumped out the car and Keith jumped out of his. He told his girlfriend to get out but she would not get out so I jumped in and we began fighting. She grabbed a handful of my hair and would not let go. No matter how much I punched and kicked, she would not let my hair go. Keith jumped in and started choking her. That pretty much put an end to the fight. She let me go and after some yelling and name-calling, I went home.

 She and Keith continued their relationship. I ended up running into my first love or should I say my first lust; the guy I lost my virginity too at age sixteen. Keith was my third partner.

This guy, who I will call Michael, would do anything for me. He really spoiled me! I figured that he was too good to be true and I was right. He had a drinking problem and so did I. The difference was that he would get very angry when he was drunk and would start yelling. It was almost as if he would totally lose his mind when he was not sober. We argued a lot. We could not get along. I had not even slept with him, at that point, and he was already about to be dismissed.

One day, at his house, after a long drawn out argument and drinking, we decided it was about time to take it to the next level. Sex! That is exactly what we did. I remember waking up and feeling very sluggish. I was hung over and so disappointed that I had slept with him. When I was drunk, it was Ok. When I sobered up, I was full of regret.

For the next few weeks, I did not want to talk to him. I just did not like him. I liked him when I was 16 but not anymore. He was annoying and to darn pushy. Either I would end up in jail for hurting him or he would for hurting me so I had to let him go.

I was at home I believe it was a Friday or Saturday night. I had just gotten out the shower when I noticed a lump in my vaginal area. It was very painful to the touch so I called the doctor. She told me it was probably nothing too serious and not to worry. Within the next few days, I had open sores all over my vaginal area and be- tween my buttocks. I was in so much pain I could barely walk. I called Keith and asked him would he take me to emergency. Though we were not sleeping together, we were cordial. He came and took me to emergency I told him what was going on and he just sat there until the doctor came in.

When the doctor came in, she took one look and immediately said it was herpes! I asked her was she sure at least six times and six times, she told me yes!

I wanted her to be wrong so bad! When Keith came in, I told him what it was. I told him that he gave it to me because he had been sleeping with that nasty girl. I did not know that herpes showed up so quickly after sex with an infected person. Keith and I had not had sex for a while but I just could not believe that Michael would be the one to give it to me. I figured that it had taken a while for it to show up. I must have got it from Keith and now had given it to Michael.

Keith was furious and ran out the hospital leaving me to drive myself home. I left the hospital in tears. I felt like I was on my deathbed; I just wanted to die!

A few days later, I called Michael and told him I needed to talk to him. I went over to his house and told him what was going on. He swore up and down it was not him. The sore on his mouth told me different. After that conversation, I never saw him again.

I was hurt and shocked. I could not believe that he had given me herpes, something that I could never get rid of!

I told my friends and my sisters and they all felt so bad for me. I took the meds that were prescribed but they did not seem to be working!

I went back to the hospital and I found out not only did I have herpes; I also had a yeast infection and bacterial Vaginosis! I was miserable. I was told not to drink while on the meds but I could not do without alcohol. I was going through a horrible time in my life.

I drank anyway and when I tell you I was sick, I was really sick! Even in all that pain, I still had to go clubbing. I did not want to miss all the fun everyone was having. After taking the meds for a while, the outbreak began clearing up. I called my godmother and my pastor and told them both what was going on. They prayed with me and encouraged me to stop sleeping around. I was scared straight there was no way I was going to sleep with anyone else.

That Sunday I went to church and told my first Lady that I had herpes. She prayed that I would be Healed. I wanted to be healed but after all, I had done, why would God heal me? That week I went to the doctor and asked her to check me to see if I still had herpes. The doctor told me, "If they told you that is what you had then you have."

I asked her could she please check me she ran test, The result NO HERPES! Gone! That is right, No herpes I was twenty-four years old then, I am twenty-eight years old now. NO HERPES! God healed me! Me, the me that said I hated Him; the one who had given up on Him, the one who dogged Him, the one who vowed not to serve Him, the alcoholic, the promiscuous one, the fighting one, the disrespectful one, the angry one, the bitter one. I could go on-and-on and on GOD HEALED ME!
I was so thankful and so happy I decided I was going back to church. I was going right back to church!

Sadly, my newfound devotion did not last. I went sex free for about four months. I began a new job, met a guy and my promiscuity started all over again.

On February 15, 2010, Keith was sent right back to Jail. He had got into it with his girlfriend and choked her. She pressed charges. With Keith being on parole, they were not playing with him. His sentence was two years in prison. I felt a bit bad, at the time, because the argument was about him helping me out.

That bad feeling only lasted a day or so. I was off To go on with my life. The guy I was dating turned out to be one of the biggest and I mean the biggest liars I had ever encountered to that time.

I did not break things off with him in the typical way. I just stopped talking to him. Mean right? So what. I did not care how he felt. I had lost anyway!

That March I received a nice sized check and Bought myself a car, some clothes for my children and I the drinks were on me.

I was very promiscuous. I stayed hot and ready. I did not care whom I gave it to as long as I was good and drunk. My life in 2010 was sex, cigarettes, clubs and alcohol.

At this time, I was hanging with some friends that I had grown up with in the church and my sisters. We would get together and have a blast. We were at the clubs drinking just about every weekend. That is right church girls!

I had already been out in the world for a while. I was never fully committed after my mother passed. I just had some new folks with me. We went out one night and

I ran into a guy that I went to school with. I immediately wanted him.

I walked up to him and hugged him. He kissed me and we were cool from there.

Crazy! Right? That is the way it was. Instead of using my, influence and leadership for good, I used it to seduce and control and boy was I good at it.

He and I clicked and within a few days, we had Slept together. After sleeping with him, I had to prepare to go to Florida that following morning.

My sisters, uncle, aunt and I went to Disney world I believe in May. We stayed a week. My kids and niece had so much fun it was certainly worth it. After returning, I called my church party girls and they no longer wanted to party. I said, "OK," and left it at that. I under- stood. They were ready to get themselves together. I was not. I went my own way and they went theirs.

I wanted to be committed to the church but I just was not ready. I was having too much fun being a bad girl. I could have easily said you guys are right. I am going to get my act together too but I am not the type to follow or do something I do not want to do because every- one else is doing it. I will only follow if it is something I want to do. Church was not my priority at that time.

I moved into a new house in July of that year. My sisters, Jo and Melissa, moved with me. My home immediately became party central! I began having sex with everyone. It did not matter. I had lost anyway!

I had nine guys in rotation. I would sleep with one on Tuesday and another on Wednesday.

Sometimes I would sleep with one in the morning and then have sex with another at night. I did not care and to be honest, I was having a blast…so I thought. I felt like I had control over my life and everyone that was in it. I used that power of control to my advantage.

If a guy called and wanted to have sex and I al-Ready had someone on schedule I would tell him exactly that. I had no filter, no respect and no dignity. Why should I? I had lost anyway! My sisters would tell me, I need to slow down, but that only made me increase!

I stayed drunk every single night! Sometimes I would get drunk as soon as I woke up in the morning! We were at the clubs Tuesdays, Wednesdays, Thursdays, Fridays, and Saturdays and Sundays that is right Mondays we were at the house but I was still drunk.

My sisters and I were well known at the clubs, especially me. I was the loud, drunk, half-naked sister. The bouncers and owners would give us free drink passes and let us move to the front of the line. I felt like a super star! I really felt like I mattered.

My sisters and I had become so cool with the one Of the club owners he would leave the club open until 4am just for us. One of us would be behind the bar making drinks while the others would be dancing on the dance floor or on the bar. We were a wild team, Jo, Melissa and I felt like we owned the world.

I slept with the owner. Did you think he was leaving the bar open just because we were pretty? Of course not! These things came with a price and I was that cheap ticket.

Chapter 7
A Motherless Child

I partied all week, every week, with or with-out my sisters. Where were the kids you ask? They were at home. I lived with them but I was never there for them. I did not want anything to happen to them but I did nothing to protect them. I wanted them to be well educated but I was just too hung over to take my son to school. I did not want them to be angry with me but I did everything to hurt them.

My Son, now nine years old spent all of his life Seeing his mother drunk. He is still trying to adjust to having a sober mother. My daughter would often act like me to get my attention but all I did was yell at her.

I was a horrible mother! I put my pleasure above My children's needs. I certainly did not take care of them. They often ate noodles and spent a lot of time with my sisters because I would wake up and leave the house without even saying a word. My kids would ask if they could come with me and I would always tell them no. I did not want to be around them, they irritated me and I felt weighed down by them.

Keith was able to get away with being a sorry father, I figured I had done enough and I was giving myself a break.

I would tell the kids to go upstairs to their room so They would be out of the way. I would not even get up in the morning to make them cereal. I was much to hang over. They could wait. Most days, I did not get up until about 2pm.

I would always put my daughter's hair up in a ponytail. I did not want to take the time to do anything more than that. Whenever I took the time to bathe them; that would be our time together for the day.

My kids did anything they could for attention. I just was neither ready, nor willing to give it to them. I never really showed my son any attention at all. He got to the point where he was scared to approach me. I would yell at him all the time. Nothing he ever did was right in my eyes. He was a boy and he looked just like his dad. This is going to sound horrible but it is the truth. I hated my own son. I would often wish he were not here or think about how it would be to have two girls and no boys.

My daughter would run up to me and hug me of-Ten. My son would stand back and ask very quietly if he could hug me. I would yell, "Hurry up!" He would run and hug me. I hated when he touched me it felt like a violation to me. I simply hated to feel genuine love from a male, even a little boy, because I was not use to it.

I could look at Jeremiah and tell he felt unloved, Rejected and lonely. Even so, I just could not bring myself to meet his needs. I was too stuck on what I needed. I felt abandoned, unloved, rejected and lonely. How could I give, someone else, what I did not have, myself. I just did not know how!

I would often tell Jeremiah, out of anger, that he was stupid, slow or that he was going to be sorry just like his daddy. I would get mad at Khrystiana, my daughter, and call her a bitch! They were only about five and seven

Year's old at the time and I been verbally abusive to them pretty much since the day they were born.

I remember bringing Jeremiah home from the hospital. That first night he cried and cried. I did not know what to do. So I picked him up and yelled, "Shut up, just shut up!" My father ran and grabbed him from me. I did not know what to do with him. I never wanted children. I could not stand kids.

That is another thing I would question…why on Gods great green earth did he allow me to have children? I could not even support myself! My son was doing horrible in school. He was stressed out and mentally just not there. I could not figure out why he was not doing his work or passing any of his tests.

Jeremiah was often picked on in school and he would come home so angry! His anger reminded me a lot of his father and I hated that. Jeremiah would call himself ugly, stupid and one time when, his dad did not come get him for his birthday, as promised, he said he did not want to be Jeremiah anymore.

Although things like that would hurt me, I was just too gone to fix any of it.

My son was truly a victim of circumstance. It was not his fault that mommy was an addict and losing her mind. It was not his fault that his father was abusive and a rapist. I made him feel as though he was the one who had done these awful things. Could you imagine carrying that weight from the time you were born until age seven?

My daughter was more out spoken than Jeremiah

She would just say how she felt and she did not care about the consequences. She would pretend to be drinking or smoking. She would dance just as if she saw me dancing on those nights when I had wild drunken parties at the house. She would take my camera and take pictures of herself trying to look like mommy.

My daughter was literally a little me and it was scary. I would tell her not to do the things she was doing but she would do them anyway because I was doing them. I was not about to stop so she figured neither would she.

I tried to teach, "Do as I say, not as I do," but that was a contradiction and even at a young age, my kids did not buy it.

One day my neighbor came over yelling at me about my kids saying they were on the roof throwing things. I knew my kids were doing things to get attention but they certainly were not on the roof. I cussed the man out as he threatened to call child protective service on me. When I went upstairs to talk to the kids Khrystiana had actually been climbing out of her window onto the roof throwing things at the neighbor's house while Jeremiah watched.

I could not believe it! You would think that I would try to get closer to my children after that but I did not. I really wanted to get away from them then. As I saw it at the time, they were the problem, not me. "I am doing the best I can," I would say. I was playing the victim and the whole time my babies were the real victims.

Another time, I can never forget, is when I was sober and had no money for alcohol. I grew very depressed I felt like a cloud was sitting on my head.

I called one of my friends and left leaving my Children at home with my little cousins. Once I got to my friend's house, she had liquor, and I got started drinking. About an hour into our impromptu drinking party, I received a phone call from my cousin. Jeremiah was trying to kill himself. Yes! My seven year-old son was trying to kill himself!

I had my friend rush me home. When I got there, Jeremiah was in tears and so was I. I asked him what happened he told me that my daughter had told him to kill himself so he was about to set his self on fire. They had actually started a fire by putting a lighter to their blanket. That day I knew that some changes needed to be made. I just did not know where to start.

Jeremiah began to have anxiety attacks. His anger was getting out of hand. He took out the anger and frustration on his sister. His attitude really changed he did not even want to hug me anymore. He grew very distant! Khrystiana would come and be around me but Jeremiah would stay in his room. The only time I really saw him was when it was time to eat. I had officially ruined my own son.

Chapter 8
All Things Must End

The father of my sister's baby, Tyrone, and I would get drunk together. He was also Keith's brother. He and I, and a lot of our other friends would get together and drink or go out. We became very close. At the time, my sister and Tyrone were not together. In fact, she could not stand him. We would all get together just about every night and drink.

I told Tyrone pretty much everything because I thought I could trust him. Tyrone had a friend named Richard. Richard was dating one of Tyrone and Keith's sisters; the sister who got me fired from my job.

They all happened to be at the house. Richard began flirting with me. Now I knew that he had crossed the line but I did not care because, as I said earlier, I sought revenge.

I flirted back and that night we had sex in my kitchen. After that, we continued to have sex. Though I knew, I was wrong I did not care. I was paying Tonya back and Keith at the same time. The way it made them feel did not really matter to me. In fact, I wanted it to bother them.

I told Tyrone about what was going on. He told Another one of their friends. He was not supposed to but he did. The other friend told Tonya.

Now at this time, I was already being accused of sleeping with the guy that Tonya cheated on Richard with. Truth is; I had not touched him. He fell asleep laying across the bottom of my bed one night after I was passed out drunk. Somehow, word of that got out. People swore up and down that I had sex with him.

Tonya hated me with a passion. She had every right to; I was sleeping with her boyfriend. The members of Tony and Keith's family began calling me on the phone to yell, cuss and go off on me. Of course, I denied everything, so did he, but we continued sleeping together.

One day, I was out with my cousin, Tyrone and a guy named Avery, who Tonya had cheated on Richard with. Avery wanted to have sex so when we reached our destination, I made a pass at Avery. He generously accepted. Before I could have sex with Avery, I had to go have sex with Richard. Richard and I had already planned to hook up so that is what I did. I had sex with Richard, went home, showered and a few hours later had sex with Avery.

Avery knew what was going on with Richard. Tyrone had opened his big mouth again but Avery did not care. He wanted me anyway.

After having sex with Avery, I decided he would
Be my number one sex partner even though I was still dealing with the tall guy I talked about earlier. I did not care I just wanted good sex and some liquor.

Avery and I began having sex on a regular basis. As you would expect, this made Richard very upset. He had started having real feelings for me. I did not want to be a serious relationship with Richard. I just wanted to use him for sex, money and liquor.

Meanwhile, I began to grow closer to Avery. To be Honest I began having feelings for him. I figured he knew

The type of chick I was. He would never settle down with me so I did what I did best. I deliberately stood him up several times. I started sleeping with someone else. I did not think the relationship had any chance of going any- where. There was no point of me telling him how I felt. I was a hoe! I am just going to keep it real and put it out there.

Avery stepped back from me for a while. My Game playing was a bit much for him. I cannot really blame him.

Mean while I spent some time with Richard and a few friends. We all went out to the club one night and had a blast. Afterward, we all spent the night at a friend's house. The next day, Tonya knocked at the door. Yup, ladies and gentlemen, she caught Richard and me together. Though nothing was happening, at that moment, but we hesitated to open the door. When we finally let her in, she went off. I remember thinking, "Yes! I got her. She is mad. I won and she lost."

Now I realize that I am the one who lost. My reputation went from "good church girl" to "nasty slut" in a matter of seven years! I had slept with forty-one men and that is just the ones I can remember.

There were several times when I woke up, in the Morning with a man next to me in bed and I did not even know how he got in my house, or how I got into his.

Not only did I kill my reputation I hurt someone being revengeful and evil. Knowing how it felt, myself, to be cheated on; to Tonya I would like to say that I am truly sorry; for all the hurt that I put you through. I pray that you are able to release and forgive me.

I felt so hated by everyone. I felt so alone and stupid. My decisions were getting worse and worse and for whatever reason. I could not stop making wrong choices.

Sometime in August, my sister Jo introduced me
To a drink called 4LOKO. At most places, you could buy two of them for just $5. When I found out that I could get drunk for only $5 I was excited. I made 4LOKO my new drink of choice. It only took two to get me wasted!

After a while, I became immune to them, I guess. I was not getting drunk so I began mixing 4LOKO with gin, vodka, beer; whatever I could get my hands on. In time, it started making me sick. I became very ill. I would sleep all day and sweat like crazy. It literally looked as if I had jumped into a pool of water. My jeans were wet my shirt was wet and I could not stay awake to save my life.

After about 4 days of feeling that way, I went to the ER. The doctor came in and told me that I was extremely ill and I would have to stay in the hospital. I later found out that I was Septic. Septic shock is a condition in which the body is fighting a severe infection that has spread via the bloodstream. If a patient becomes "septic," they will likely have low blood pressure leading to poor circulation and lack of perfusion of vital tissues and organs. This condition is termed "shock" and is sometimes referred to as "septic shock," when an infection is the cause of shock. This condition can develop as a result either of the body's own defense system or from toxic substances made by the infecting agent (such as a bacteria, virus, or fungus).

The doctor told me that I had made it to the hospital just in time. A urinary tract infection had gotten into
my blood stream. I could have died. I was very thankful that I made it. Once again, God had come through for me but I still

had no desire to serve Him; at least not completely.

My pastors came up to the hospital to see me and prayed that God would heal me. I am not sure I ever gave this testimony but the doctor came in after doing a cat scan and some other test and showed me some stone looking things that were inside my kidneys.

The next day they came in, after retesting me and the stones were gone! That is right gone! God kept looking out for me in spite of my rebellion. I had been healed, again! Wow! God did say He was married to the back-slider and he proved it time after time.

After spending five long days in the hospital, I Was finally released. When I got home, I did not drink for about four days. My sobriety did not last very long. Around day five, I was right back to where I started. The only thing that changed was my drink of choice. I did not go back to 4LOKO! Instead, I went straight to 1800 Silver; another poor decision.

In October of 2010, I went to the club with a bunch of my friends. I believe it was nine of us. My best friend, Julie, and I had on pink lingerie. It was a promotional event for breast cancer awareness. That night, I told all the girls that when I go to the club I am a V.I.P.!

Usually, when my sisters and I would go to the clubs, we received V.I.P. treatment. I assumed we would get the same treatment that night. I was wrong!

The bouncers were very rude and mean to me that Night. They would not allow us to cut to the front of the line as usual. I wondered what was up, but I let it go; maybe it was just a bad night. When we went in, we went straight to the bar to get a drink. We got our drinks and started to walk away from the bar. One of the girls accidently bumped into a guy and half his drink spilled all over him.

He was not pleased, to say the least. We apologized and kept walking. The next thing we know, we were wet! The guy had thrown the rest of his drink on us.

Usually I would go into fight mode but we wanted to stay and have fun so I told the bouncer what had happened. To my surprise, he told us to leave! I said, "What? Are you guys serious?" He said, "Yes," and began escorting us out of the building.

I was furious. I figured that since we were being thrown out why not go out with a bang! On the way out, I saw the guy who had thrown the liquor on us. I began punching him in his head. The bouncer then picked me up and threw me out. A police officer, standing there, outside the door, yelled at me and ordered me to get across the street.

I was already on my way so I did not understand why he was telling me to do what I was already doing. Suddenly, the officer pushed me so hard I flew in the middle of the street and almost fell. I got up and pushed him back! Two more cops appeared, seemingly, out of nowhere. They pinned me to the ground, cuffed me and put me into their truck, under arrest!

My friends were yelling and screaming because the officers were being extremely rough with me. I had on lingerie and six inch heels. I am six feet tall but only about one hundred forty-five pounds. The amount of force they were using was unnecessary!

While in the police car, I began crying and begging them to let me go. The officer kept saying I should not have pushed him. I kept saying, "Well; you pushed me first." I was too drunk to even pretend that I was thinking clearly.

Once we got to the police station, they had to book me. I was not about to cooperate. I would not open my hand so they could get my fingerprints. I made jokes about everything. Finally, an officer was able to get my fingerprints and they put me in the holding cell.

After being held down and raped for ten hours, I was a bit claustrophobic. I thought I was going to lose my mind locked in that small space! I could not be still. On top of that, I had blown a 1.6 on the breathalyzer. I was wasted! I felt like I was going to die if I did not get out of there soon. I was making faces at the camera and lifting up my middle finger at whoever was on the other end, watching the monitor. I was very frustrated.

The officer came in and told me that once I sobered up they would let me go home. I believed him and sat there as best I could until the guys across from me, in the other holding cell, yelling out lewd sexual comments.

That really made me mad. There I was, in public, in lingerie but I did not care. No man was going to talk to me that way. So, I got up and started going off! I started yelling back. After about five minutes, the officer came in and they told me I was going to jail.

I said, "But I thought you said I was going home?" He said nothing and handed me over to a different officer; an officer that I knew from previous contacts with the police.

I cried like a baby while in the car on the way to the Oakland county jail. The officers at the station would not allow me the "one phone call" that is supposed to be the right of anyone in custody. The officer who was transporting me to the county jail allowed me to use his cell phone.

I called my father and told him what had happened. He did not want me in jail. He asked the officer could he come get me but the officer told him no. I would have to stay the night in the Oakland lock up.

Once at Oakland County, I was very uncooperative. The female officers kept telling me that it would be smart for me to calm down. They said I could end up in jail longer if I did not quit. As mad as I was, I went from 10 to zero very fast. Jail was not a place for me and I was ready to go.

I spent a sleepless night in jail. Once they woke me up, at 5 AM, I was ready to go.

"Who eats breakfast at 5am?" I thought. I was so angry I did not know what to do with myself. All I could think about was sex, a cigarette and alcohol. I needed it!

As the hours passed the more frustrated I became. I felt so lonely in that cell. Even when they let us out to socialize, I felt alone. Jail is a cold, lonely horrible place to be.

I sat around and heard some of the other women's stories. At that moment, a strong desire to help them came over me.

"How could I?" I thought, "When I can barely help myself?"

It was finally time for me to be arraigned. I was so happy when the judge told me they would let me out on a personal bond. I went back to my cell and about three hours later I heard, "Gulley." I looked up, "Yes." "You are going home." I ran out of that cell!

I was hungry, angry, happy, frustrated, mad, sad, Depressed and annoyed all at once. As soon as I got home, I headed straight for the cigarettes and the liquor. I got drunk.

I partied hard for the next few weeks because I knew once that letter came from court they were going to stop me.

I began hanging with a girl that I met through my cousin. We grew very close. She was a lesbian and I was straight but I did not care about her sexuality. My sisters were not hanging out with me as much and all my friends were, pretty much, gone. I just wanted a friend.

She and I would go party all the time. We stayed drunk. I was happy to have someone with me that was on the same page I was. She and I hung around each oth- er a good while before things started getting out of hand. You see, she started sleeping with my cousin and my family started calling me gay. I was angry that my cousin never spoke up. I assumed she must of been ashamed so I didn't say anything either.

I was not brought up around this side of the famly. I was not as close to everyone as she was so, what they thought of me was not as important to me as I am sure it was to her.

Right after that rumor got started, another rumor got started. People were saying I wanted to jump my own cousin. It simply was not true. I was very hurt; my own cousin came after me with a knife all because of a lie that another cousin had told.

After that, I was accused of stealing my aunt's keys to get to her money. I was devastated. It seemed like everything was happening all at once and I did not know what to do. No one believed me when I denied everything that I was accused of so I stopped going around my family. I figured they did not care about me. What was the point of being around them? They pushed me completely away and away is where I went.

Chapter 9
Getting My Life Back

My letter for court arrived. I went and was given eleven months' probation with a delayed sentence. A delayed sentence means that as long as I do not get in any trouble, I would not receive the penalty. If I got into trouble, however, the judge would throw the book at me. The charge was assault on an officer, a felony if convicted.

While on probation, I still got drunk. I could not Quit! I never wanted to admit it at that time that I had a problem so I denied it even though, deep inside, I knew there was something wrong. I was placed in an anger management program, a woman's group and counseling.

Counseling was very helpful. I felt like I had an outlet. The counselor allowed me to let it all out.

Every time I went I cried because I was so broken. I cried about my mother. I cried about the rape. I cried about my promiscuity. I cried about my dad, my children, my house, my family, everything.

I was depressed. I was falling apart. Every time I Attempted to leave the alcohol, alone it seemed as if a huge weight sat on my shoulders so I continued to drink even though I did not want to. I could not help it.

I had a real addiction I could not cope without a Drink. Sometimes my body would hurt if I had no alcohol. I was on edge all the time anything would and could set me off. I would get angry at what people would call small things, but they were big to me. For instance, if someone touched my stuff I would blow up. I felt that so much had already been taken from me. I was not going

To let anyone take anything else. Touching anything that belonged to me was a danger zone. When I blew, people around me would say that I had no reason to. It made me feel misunderstood. You see, in my mind I had every rea- son to be angry and blowing up was actually letting them off easy.

I hated it when people lied about me. To be honest, I decided to stop fighting against the lies and gossip. I have always been very transparent. I do not mind al- lowing people to see my mess-ups or my flaws.

I know not everyone thinks the way I think. As I see it, it is human to mess up sometimes. To pretend that I do not have any faults or to hide my flaws is just plain deceit. When you are transparent all people can do is lie on you. If they want to harm you, they must make up things. There is nothing hidden for them to dig up, It's already out there.

I tell all my own business. I do not need any help. I would get very upset when lied on. The thing that I hated most was when people chose to believe the mess and lies.

Anything that made me feel good I took it to the extreme from weed, alcohol, clubs and sex. After having sex with all those men, I still wanted more. I had sex with two guys at once, Avery being one of them. I even had a desire to sleep with women but never went that far.

When I smoked weed it went from one blunt a day to four to five a day. Drinking went from two cups a day to a fifth or more a day.

As for sex, well, I could do that all day and night. I Was a full-blown mess. I know I keep saying that but I Can't think of a better way to describe what I was like at that miserable point in my life.

If I did not say it out my mouth then it probably is not

true. I am very honest and I am not the scary type.
I would also get upset when others would call themselves telling my business. It was not that I was trying to hide anything but as I said; I would put it out there myself. It is hypocritical to be willing to put someone else's troubles out there and not be willing to put your own business out there. It is hypocritical and cowardly.

The only time you hear about what they did is
Through a rumor that they would deny; that always
Made me go into fight mode. Even to this day, it really galls me. I am just being honest. I do not like when people try to hide their mess while putting yours on blast.

These may seem like small matters but they were
Major problems in my mind. They were among the main things I brought up in counseling.

I walked in offense. I was the wrong person to mess with. I put on a very hard front because I felt like I only had me to protect me. Do not get me wrong I was not a punk then, nor am I now but I just was not as hard as I portrayed myself to be.

In late November, I began going to modeling school. I was excited. I felt like I was alive again. I was back in church and I was easing up some on the drinking and partying.

I graduated from modeling school in January 2011. I had not given up drinking altogether, but I was no longer getting drunk every day. I really felt like I was on my way. I had completely stopped sleeping with everyone except Avery and I was finally finding some of happiness.

Anger management and the women's groups taught me a lot. I was slowly but surely making some changes.

My home life was even improving. At one point, I
Kept my house a nasty mess. That is how I felt on the in- side

and it showed everywhere on the outside. That all ended when I saw a mouse, I am horrified of mice! My sisters and I began seeing them everywhere. It was the worst thing ever! I became stressed out all over again. Everything I had learned in counseling went out the window.

    I went right back to drinking heavy and partying. Since I was banned from all the clubs for 11 months, I had to do my partying at home.

    I was finally able to move out of that house in July of 2011. I was excited and I felt at peace. I really loved the new home but that did not last long at all.

    When I first moved, I did not drink. I kept the House clean and I was happy. I had not seen Avery those first few weeks but once I did see him, we got something to drink and the negative behavior started all over again. Was the problem Avery? No! When you have an addiction, or just bad habit, you associate it with things or even people.

    For example: I would never be sober while having Sex and every time I was with Avery we got drunk and had sex. Every time Avery came over I expected liquor and sex. That is what I got. Liquor, sex and cigarettes all

Went hand in hand to me. You cannot have one without the other and they were all addictions for me.

    Avery ended up moving in with me. That whole month I stayed drunk! I would drink so much I would wake up drunk the next morning. Hangovers were my friend until I learned how to take care of them.

    I was right back to square one before I knew it. I had people over just about every night getting high. I did not smoke weed at the time but I drank and stayed drunk.

I hated who I was and I did not want to be that way anymore. I knew of only one person that I could talk to who would tell me "the truth without judgment. That was my pastor, Gregory Heathman. I put up a status on Facebook saying that I needed my pastor. He responded and said. "I am still awake, just call." It was very late that night. How many pastors do you know would do that! I dare to say not many!

I did not call him that night because I was drunk And I did not want to sound crazy on the phone. The next day I called him and told him what was going on and he just flat out told me, as he had in the past, to stop drinking.

I thought that he was crazy because hello, I am an Addict! I cannot just stop man. I gave him reason after reason why I could not stop and he still kept telling me to stop. My pastor is not one to say any ole thing just to shut you up. He will keep it real and give it to you straight so I knew that if he was telling me to just quit, knowing that I was an addict, that he must have known something that I did not.

One day sometime into the second week of Au- gust, a few days after talking to my pastor, I had no money, no way to get any and neither did Avery. I was depressed, sad, scared, annoyed, and angry all at the same time. Sobriety was not where I wanted to be. I had eight years of emotions in my head.

That day Avery looked at me and saw all I was going through and said, "Christine why don't you just quit drinking? I already had my thoughts of quitting after talking to my pastor so once Avery said it, I decided to quit.

The next couple of days were very hard for me. I prayed a lot and asked for a lot of forgiveness. I felt bad for ignoring God for so long. At that point, in my life, I needed him. Avery really encouraged me not to drink. It was not easy at times, I would want to. He was there for me through it all that is how I knew there was something different about him. If I were in his shoes, I would have been gone. He had seen everything I was doing and going through yet he stuck by me.

I decided that I needed additional help so I checked myself into outpatient rehab. When I went, I was ten days sober and my counselor was shocked. She said that she had never met anyone who was able to stay clean without help for that long. I thought wow its only ten days! I later learned that most alcoholics go through major issues in a matter of hours while trying to recover. I knew that it was nothing but God.

As I said earlier that my pastor knew something I Did not. He knew that I could stop drinking with the power of God! I was looking at my own strength he was looking at the awesome power of God. With God's awesome strength, not my own, I was able to make it to ten days of sobriety.

Rehab was such a blessing to me. I learned so much from the time spent around people that were going through the same thing I was going through. I had eight years of issues that I now have to deal with. Things I tried to fight with anger and drown in alcohol. It was not easy. I cried a lot. To be honest, sometimes still cry. I cannot even begin to tell you how many times I cried while writing this book! Healing is a process and sup- pressing pain just makes that process longer but with the help of God you can get through it.

I would have nightmares that my kid's dad was Coming to kill me. Sometimes I would wake up and think he was there, in the house!

Avery was jarred out of his sleep many nights as I woke up in a panic because of the night terrors I was experiencing. I was so afraid. I thought I was losing my mind. I could not sleep at night. I felt as if I was going to die.

    I would get in the shower and hurry to get out be-Because I would imagine that someone was going to suddenly pull the curtain back and kill me.

    I was afraid to walk anywhere alone. I did not
Even want to be home alone.

    It was hard to even stand in my kitchen and wash
Dishes because with my face toward the sink, my back would be turned toward the open room. It would feel as if someone was standing in the room over me. I was in total agony.

    I ended up in the hospital a few times from with drawl sickness. I was put on anti-depressants, Ado van and muscle relaxers. I was dead!

    I would sit on the couch in the same spot and stare
At the wall all day, every day. Avery would come, pick up my dead arm and it would just fall back into its place. He complained that I was a bore and a mess. I knew he was right but the medication made me feel less afraid. I was able to sleep at night.

Chapter 10
Freedom

Around this time, I was all the way in the church. I still smoked cigarettes but I knew that in time God would deliver me from them. That August I shared the poem that is at the end of this chapter I Have Been There Done That, Now What?

I told my whole story in one poem and it felt Good. I began counseling with my first lady on top of going to rehab. I knew that I needed help and a change needed to take place.

Let me stop right there. When we get so focused on playing the victim and looking at everyone else, we cannot be free.

I could have blamed everyone for the mess I was In but I knew it would do me no good. I had to get honest with myself.

Most of the things I was going through I brought upon myself. I told my first lady everything and she began praying for me. When I tell, you God set me free, HE SET ME FREE!

I was delivered from abuse, addiction, insanity, Hurt, depression, fear, promiscuity, perversion, shame, abandonment and so many other things that had a hold on me.

People wonder how I got so far so fast. Well, let Me tell you. The Bible says, "Therefore confess your sins to each other and pray for each other so that you may be healed. The prayer of a righteous man is powerful and effective" (James 5:16). That is all I did. It didn't take any Anything special to be free. All you have to do is confess. I have never been the type, even as a child, to throw the rock and hide my hand. I do not get along well with those who do.

I love to see people healed and set free. I love to evangelize. I will sit down and talk with you all night about an issue or pray. I will not however play games with people. If you want freedom, I will, with the help of God, help get you there.

You have to be honest to be free there is no way Around it. Ask yourself a question, what is it that you have not released? What are you hiding? What have you suppressed and tucked away? What is still there, down deep within, where only the Lord can dig it out?
It is a very painful process to look deep within yourself and bring to the surface things that had been buried.

You may have to risk being vulnerable to be free. People often tell me, I am too open. I am too transparent. You know what I say, "So what! I'm free!"

Trying to be Mr. or Mrs. Goody Two Shoes will get you nowhere. Why would you want to hide the fact that you are human? We all make mistakes. We have all fallen short of the glory of God.

Some of you will not even confess to God and he already knows all things. You cannot hide from him!

I rebuke the hand of the enemy. I command the devil to take his hand off you. I command that you be made free, in your mind, in the name of Jesus!

You can tell God anything! You are not too far- gone. You can be free! LOOK AT ME!

If you got to this page then you know I was a mess and God still said, "Come here baby, let me clean you up. I have some work for you to do."

If he did it for me, He can and He will do it for you!

Did I get free over night? No way! As I said before, I am still healing from things. I am still in the process. Have I fallen along the way? I have had to go to my pastor and confess a few times. I have went off on people, cussed them out, drank alcohol, been to the club, fornicated, talked about people, been involved in gossip all type of nonsense.

I still battle with going off on people. I had a very bad attitude. God is still working on me. I can honestly say I am nowhere near, what I use to be. Maybe by the time you read this book I will not be struggling with that problem at all. I hope that by then God will be working on another one of my many flaws.

Why am I telling you this? Because I want you to know that, it is not about instant perfection. I sense in my spirit that some of you are not OK with being imperfect. There is only one who is perfect and without sin and His name is JESUS!

You will stress yourself out trying to be something you can never be. Stop trying to please everyone. God never meant for us to be people pleasers.

If Jesus pleased people, He would not have died on that cross. Mary, like any other mother, did not want to watch her baby die. If He would have stayed to please her, we all would be doomed! What does that tell you? Trying to please people instead of God hurts not only you, but others as well. Someone needs you and you and I need Jesus. God made you the way that you are because he knew that you could get the job done just being you! Be encouraged.

I had to completely separate myself from people for a season. God had to take some people out of my life. I do not have an issue now with removing myself from negative people. I had to learn the hard way that I cannot be around everyone and everything.

Not everyone can go where you are going. I struggled with people talking about me because I had changed. I went through a period about a year ago when people were starting false rumors and spreading lies. I wanted to give up and quit after talking to my pastor numerous times and hearing preached word after preached word, I hung in there.

Stop allowing the enemy to influence you to stay away from church because people there are messy or fake. The church is like a hospital sick people go there. God is the doctor and the pastors and ministers are His tools. People in the church need help just like you do.

Yes, it hurts when a brother or sister in the church wounds you. I have been wounded numerous times. My mouth and attitude have wounded others as well. I am trying to help you eliminate the excuses so you can take one step closer towards your freedom.

Get out of yourself. It is not now, never has been and never will be, about you. Humble yourself you did not wake yourself up God did it. You are not able to read this book by your own power it is Gods power.

God deserves His glory! What would I look like telling you that I delivered myself from being raped? I spared my own life. Huh? No honey it was by the grace and mercy of Almighty God!

Do not ever take God's glory; ever; you put your-self in a dangerous spot when you do that. God is a jealous God. He hates when we give to ourselves, or others, that which is due to him. You would be too!

I go through many things still because God is shaping me and making me into the woman of God that he desires for me to be. I am one of God's chosen; I have had to go through a lot of hurt and pain even in the church because God is trying to take all the old Christine out so that everything that comes out of the new Chris- tine is pure. You may have to go through the same thing. It is not to break you. It is to make you.

Today I serve in my church as President of the worship and praise team. I am Co- president of the worship arts department, I am an aspiring minister and member of a ministry we call A.W.M. productions. I have taken over as president of Spirit, Soul and Body, a ministry birthed through my mother.

I am blessed beyond measure. God has done things for me not even I can believe.

God immediately began changing me. I have al- ways been able to sing but God turned my singing into anointed worship. Until this day, I am still amazed at the sound that comes out of my mouth. I am very humbled that God would use me after all I have done. Within months of my recovery, my First Lady, Dr. Patricia Heathman, told me that she saw a preaching gift in me. A short while later I was sharing the Word for the first time. I was shocked. I am not ordained yet. I am an aspiring minister. At our church, an "aspiring minister" is one who has acknowledged the call of God upon his or her life and is in the training process. Even that boggles my mind. Who would have thought, two years ago, that Christine Gulley would be preaching to anyone?

On November 29, 2012, I married Avery! Yup, that is right; he put a ring on it! I remember telling some old friends that he was not the one. I did not want him. We had been through too much. Avery and I would fight like cats and dogs. I am not talking just verbal either!

Avery gave his life to the Lord. Once God and my

pastor approved, we got married.

Let me encourage the person who was just like me! I allowed the enemy to tell me that because of my past no one would marry me. I told people that. Who would want a woman who had sex with 41 men...plus!

I am still amazed that I am married and my husband is good to me! He took my babies in and treats them as if they are his own. He provides for me, for them and for our beautiful home.

I am able to focus fully on my ministry, without a Care in the world because of him. In spite of my past, he Loves me and he cherishes me. He knew that I was transparent when he met me and he allows me to be who I am. If it were not for him, I would not have been able to share a lot of my struggle with you. I thank God for my husband and I love him dearly.

In less than 2 years God has turned my life around And I know that he can and will do it for you. Just be honest, let go, submit to God, totally. Give your heart to him. Allow him to use you. Share your testimony! It is not complimentary for me to tell you all these things. It is however to God's glory. He gets all the glory and the honor out of my life. Take the steps I mentioned earlier and watch God turn your life from trial to testimony!

Been There, Done That Been there, done that!
I have been in the streets, no sense, no shelter and nothing to eat!

I am not ashamed to say it. Yeah, I sat in that seat!

Smoked weed, brain was so fried it is a wonder I am still alive!
I would sit and cry, thinking about suicide. Been there, done that now what?
There were times when I would be so drunk

Yup! When asked, I could put up a front. I am not even going to stunt.

I would be too hung over to come to church.
I slept around, not with one, not with two but
With at least forty-one men and that is the truth!

I felt that if I did not they would take it. One more rape I knew I could not make it.

Been there, done that now what?
I have had thoughts of prostitution. I
Thought selling my body would be a solution.

I searched for love in all the wrong places. Diagnosed with herpes
I knew no one would want me but God healed me. The devil had me scared to share that part of my story.

Been there, done that, now what?

Through myself a pity party on the daily, will I do something about it?

I do not know maybe! People call me crazy it is my life;

You cannot tell me nothing if I decide to sit around and be lazy!

Been there done that no what?
O yeah I was at the club shaking my butt

And drinking my cup until someone passed me a laced blunt!

Still do not remember what happened that day did not even thank God for allowing me to see another day.

Stuck in a box of depression, oppression, obsession Oh my God where is my blessing in this awful life lesson? I am tired of stressing!

Been there, done that, now what?

God who? He takes too long

I may as well continue in my wrong!

Why we would, he help me after all I have done?

SHOOT! I am about to go get me some.

My mom is dead! Yeah I am mad! Full of anger and you want

to talk to me about a savior when he did not even save her! That is the excuse I used for my anger! Been there, done that, now what?
Two kids, on welfare, baby daddy sure aint
There! Now you know that aint fair!

Sometimes things get so hard I want to go outside and ask, "Is there any change you can spare"

I put myself out there to let you know that I have been there and that I care you do not have to walk alone all hope is not gone no one is perfect and salvation in not a contest we all can make progress! Be blessed!

Made in the USA
Monee, IL
01 April 2022